Interfaith Dialogue and Peacebuilding

Interfaith Dialogue and Peacebuilding

DAVID R. SMOCK, EDITOR

UNITED STATES INSTITUTE OF PEACE PRESS
Washington, D.C.

UNITED STATES INSTITUTE OF PEACE
1200 17th Street NW, Suite 200
Washington, DC 20036-3011

© 2002 by the Endowment of the United States Institute of Peace

First published 2002

Printed in the United States of America

The paper used in this publication meets the minimum requirements of American National Standards for Information Science—Permanence of Paper for Printed Library Materials, ANSI Z39.48-1984.

Library of Congress Cataloging-in-Publication Data
Interfaith dialogue and peacebuilding / David R. Smock, editor.
    p. cm.
    Includes bibliographical references and index.
    ISBN 1-929223-35-8 (pbk. : alk. paper)
    1. Religions—Relations. 2. Peace—Religious aspects—Christianity.
I. Smock, David R.

BL410.I548 2002
291.1'72—dc21

2002024265

Contents

FOREWORD
Richard H. Solomon   vii

ACKNOWLEDGMENTS   xi

INTRODUCTION
David R. Smock   3

PART I   *Promises and Challenges of Interfaith Dialogue*   13

1. The Miracles of Transformation through Interfaith
   Dialogue: Are You a Believer?
   Mohammed Abu-Nimer   15

2. The Use of the Word and Its Limits: A Critical
   Evaluation of Religious Dialogue as Peacemaking
   Marc Gopin   33

3. Building Bridges for Interfaith Dialogue
   Jaco Cilliers   47

PART II   *The Practice of Dialogue: Case Studies*   61

4. American Jews, Christians, and Muslims Working
   Together for Peace in the Middle East
   Ronald Young   63

5. Contributions of Interfaith Dialogue to Peacebuilding
   in the Former Yugoslavia
   David Steele   73

6. Mitigation in Northern Ireland: A Strategy for
   Living in Peace When Truth Claims Clash
   Joseph Liechty   89

PART III   *Peacebuilding through Interfaith Organizations*   103

7. Religion and Interfaith Conflict: Appeal of
   Conscience Foundation
   Arthur Schneier   105

8. The United Religions Initiative at Work
   Charles Gibbs   115

   CONCLUSION
   David R. Smock   127

   CONTRIBUTORS   133

   INDEX   137

Foreword

Despite the malign intentions of the terrorists directing the attacks of September 11, 2001, the world today is not wracked by war between Muslims, on the one side, and Christians and Jews, on the other side. Nor, despite the stated objectives of Osama bin Laden, is the world convulsed by a "clash of civilizations." If anything, conflicts within the Islamic world seem more likely. So far at least, peoples of very different faiths, and the governments that represent them, have largely rejected the idea that their religion and culture compel them to struggle for supremacy over, or defense against, other religions and other cultures. Few in the Islamic world greeted with joy the attacks on New York and Washington, D.C.; most were appalled or fearful that Muslims would be singled out for blame. Sympathy for the victims of Osama's violence and support for efforts to eradicate the al Qaeda terrorist network have come from all continents and faith traditions.

Yet, while *global* religious war has not erupted, *more localized* conflict between adherents of different religions remains as pervasive, and as bloody, as ever. As David Smock notes at the outset of this slim but challenging and ultimately encouraging volume, "With regrettable frequency, religion is a factor in international conflict. Rarely is religion the principal cause of conflict, even when the opposing groups . . . are differentiated by religious identity. But religion is nevertheless a contributing factor to conflict in places as widely scattered as Northern Ireland, the Middle East, the Balkans, Sudan, Indonesia, and Kashmir." It is both sad and instructive to note that while the events of September 11 have made this book especially timely, it would have been just as relevant at almost any point in recent years. The history of the association between religion and conflict, both civil and international, is very long, but the ending of the Cold War and the consequent upsurge in "identity conflicts"—waged between groups defined by factors such as ethnicity, race, and religion—has given new emphasis to that association. Nothing and no one is immune from the effects of this closer relationship. NATO, for example, a profoundly secular organization whose member-states encompass several religions, fought the first war in its fifty-year history to protect Muslims who were being evicted from Kosovo by Orthodox Serbs!

There is, however, a bright light amid the human and material devastation wrought by these identity conflicts. While religion can and does contribute to violent conflict, it also can be a powerful factor in the struggle for peace and reconciliation. Religion can be a positive influence in numerous ways. Theologically, for instance, all three of the Abrahamic faiths set store in mercy and forgiveness, qualities that are indispensable in seeking a resolution to long-standing and deeply entrenched conflicts. Their clergy, especially in strife-torn regions, usually carry great authority and are present at all levels of society, thus enabling them to be unusually effective advocates of dialogue and reconciliation. Furthermore, for all their differences, there is much that people of faith have in common—not the least of which, of course, is spirituality itself. The recognition of a shared concern to develop "honest, loving, and holistic relationships with God and neighbor" (to quote from Charles Gibbs's chapter in this book) can form the basis for the rebuilding of constructive relationships destroyed by violence.

The peacemaking potential of religion can be powerfully expressed in unilateral actions by one or another of the sides in a conflict. However, as *Interfaith Dialogue and Peacebuilding* clearly demonstrates, when two or more faiths come together to explore or promote the possibility of peace, the effects can be especially potent. The contributors to this volume focus on the increasingly common practice of dialogue between adherents of different faiths who are concerned to restore peace to their fractured communities. Such interfaith dialogue can take a wide variety of forms, ranging from joint appeals by high-level religious leaders for an end to fighting, to attempts to develop mutual understanding and the recognition of shared values and interests, to grassroots efforts to encourage repentance and promote reconciliation.

As the reader will discover, interfaith dialogue is a difficult, often painful, endeavor. It brings no guarantee of success. The authors—who are not only scholars but also practitioners of interfaith dialogue—acknowledge the limitations of this approach, identify its shortcomings, and point out that it should not be attempted without careful preparation and a clearly defined purpose. But they also illuminate its possibilities and

illustrate its achievements. Interfaith dialogue can enhance mutual awareness, foster joint activities, and even transform relationships between
members of warring groups.

If we are to capitalize on religion's ability to ameliorate or reconcile
the very conflicts that it has helped to inspire, we must heed both the
caveats and the endorsements. We must not let ourselves be carried away
by unrealistic expectations or dismayed by unavoidable failures. David
Smock and his fellow authors have approached this volume with just such
an outlook. Worried by "the fact that we have encountered many instances
of interfaith sessions degenerating into shouting matches," they have been
inspired to write a "book with recommendations on how to make interfaith sessions productive."

The same concern to learn and disseminate the lessons of what works
—and what does not—in the field of faith-based peacemaking underpins all
the projects supported by the Religion and Peacemaking Initiative of the
United States Institute of Peace. In addition to producing this book, the
initiative has organized public workshops that have examined Islamic, Catholic, Jewish, and Mennonite approaches to peacemaking, as well as peacemaking by faith-based NGOs. The initiative also has ongoing field projects
in Macedonia and Bosnia, and offers information and counsel to faith-based
organizations about opportunities for peacemaking.

The workshops have yielded three published reports (*Islamic Perspectives on Peace and Violence, Faith-Based NGOs and International Peacebuilding,* and *Catholic Contributions to International Peace*) that complement
a range other publications by the United States Institute of Peace. For
instance, the Institute's earlier initiative on Religion, Ethics, and Human
Rights led to books on Ukraine, Sri Lanka, and Islamic activism. The
Institute's Grant Program and Jennings Randolph fellowship program have
also supported studies that examine conflicts in which religion plays an important role (for instance, Ted Robert Gurr's *Peoples versus States* and John
Darby's *The Effects of Violence on Peace Processes*) and that analyze innovative
efforts to resolve those conflicts (for example, John Paul Lederach's *Building
Peace* and John Wallach's *The Enemy Has a Face*).

As the Institute's various projects attest, faith-based peacemaking
efforts are playing an increasingly significant role on the international
stage. We at the Institute hope that books such as *Interfaith Dialogue and*

Peacebuilding will help to make those efforts more effective. The events of September 11 and the subsequent international response have not generated a worldwide war of religion, but they have underlined the dangers of allowing zealots to yoke religious passions to political causes, and the advantages of harnessing religious commitment to the cause of peace.

RICHARD H. SOLOMON, PRESIDENT
UNITED STATES INSTITUTE OF PEACE

Acknowledgments

I am grateful to Dan Snodderly, Nigel Quinney, David Little, Scott Appleby, John Paul Lederach, and my wife, Lois Stovall, for their review of the manuscript and the helpful revisions they suggested. I am also indebted to my program assistant, Renata Stuebner.

Interfaith Dialogue and Peacebuilding

Introduction

David R. Smock

WITH REGRETTABLE FREQUENCY, religion is a factor in international conflict. Rarely is religion the principal cause of conflict, even when the opposing groups, such as Protestants and Catholics in Northern Ireland, are differentiated by religious identities. But religion is nevertheless a contributing factor to conflict in places as widely scattered as Northern Ireland, the Middle East, the Balkans, Sudan, Indonesia, and Kashmir. Hans Küng has asserted that the "most fanatical and cruelest political struggles are those that have been colored, inspired, and legitimized by religion."[1]

During the fall of 2001 there unfolded what appeared to be a clear clash of religiously based civilizations. The presumed perpetrators of the events of September 11 declared that the Muslim world was at war with the worlds of Christianity and Judaism. As the *Economist* described it, "Making artful use of history, theology and current geopolitics, [Osama bin Laden] has, in effect, urged all the world's billion-odd Muslims to bury their internal differences and consider themselves at war with all the world's Christians and Jews. In his efforts to galvanize and unite fellow Muslims, he has made a careful choice of the message," focusing on the conflict over holy sites in Israel/Palestine, labeling the entire Western world as "Crusaders," and reminding Muslims of past glories in what is now Spain when the Muslims were in control, before being displaced by Christians.[2]

In response Western leaders tried to make clear that the fight against terrorism is not a campaign by Christians and Jews against Muslims and Islam. Christians and Jews in the West scrambled to comprehend why a portion of the Muslim world support the radical rhetoric of bin Laden and, in turn, why the West is so deeply hated and distrusted by bin Laden and his supporters.

In a column in the *New York Times* in November 2001, Thomas Friedman wrote, "If 9/11 was indeed the onset of World War III, we have to understand what this war is about. We're not fighting to eradicate 'terrorism.' Terrorism is just a tool. We're fighting to defeat an ideology: religious totalitarianism." Friedman quoted Rabbi David Hartman: "The opposite of religious totalitarianism is an ideology of pluralism—an ideology that embraces religious diversity and the idea that my faith can be nurtured without claiming exclusive truth."[3]

Many Christians and Jews, readily admitting their ignorance of Islam, sought to understand Islam better and wondered how radical Islamist rhetoric fit with more mainstream Islamic theology and ideology. Some were prepared to take this radical rhetoric as symptomatic of a widespread pathology within Islam that made Muslims generally suspect as purveyors of hatred and terrorist acts.

Christians and Jews with a more balanced perspective on Islam and the Muslim world recognized an immediate need to engage the Muslim world more successfully than they had done in the past. Interfaith dialogue became fashionable in many U.S. churches, synagogues, and mosques. These efforts sought to increase mutual understanding and to reduce the likelihood of widespread interfaith animosity and conflict. Organizations such as the United States Institute of Peace, the World Conference on Religion and Peace, and the Community of Sant'Egidio have identified an urgent need to convene Christians, Muslims, and Jews internationally to help defuse tension and forestall wider religious conflict.

The United States Institute of Peace has advocated vigorous dialogue among religious leaders from the United States and Europe (Christian, Jewish, and Muslim) and from the Islamic world. The multiple purposes of this dialogue are to

◆ produce greater understanding of the varieties of Islamic thought;

◆ support moderate Islamic scholars who are prepared to delegitimate terrorism;

◆ help ensure that U.S. action against terrorism is not directed against Islam and Muslims in an undifferentiated manner;

◆ provide a vehicle for religious leaders in the Middle East to advocate an end to violence and to reach a peaceful resolution of the Israeli-Palestinian conflict;

◆ engage influential religious leaders in the constructive development of policies relating to international peacemaking; and

◆ escape mutual demonization.

While religiously motivated terrorism has provided the most compelling impetus for interfaith dialogue, the momentum toward greater attention to interfaith dialogue was building well before the fall of 2001. Although the prestige of the participants and the press coverage were out of proportion to the effectiveness of the event, the UN Summit of Religious and Spiritual Leaders in August 2000 gave international interfaith dialogue considerable public attention. The principal background paper to the summit stated: "The particular challenges of the Summit are several. . . . Leaders of different traditions, worldview, and patterns of belief are invited to confront common problems that no one religious community can solve, or even meaningfully address, on its own. In addition, leaders are invited to share honestly and sympathetically with one another the impediments and hardships that conspire to thwart all pure forms of religious endeavor. Still again, amicable discourse requires working out a mode of deliberation that begins to replace sufferance and coexistence with respect and interaction, and not only among the traditions, but within them as well."[4] This background paper cited several topics of special concern for the summit, namely, treatment of religious minorities, conflicting interpretations of religious freedom, force and nonviolence, religion and human rights, religion and public life, and coping with the aftermath of violence. It asserted: "At a summit designed to change, rather than simply lament, existing patterns of violence and intolerance, religious and spiritual leaders may be encouraged to do more than affirm pious platitudes about how much they and their respective traditions favor peace.

On such an occasion, new thinking is called for which involves honesty and self-criticism, as well as expressions of appreciation, regarding the traditions represented."5

At its most basic, interfaith dialogue is a simple concept: persons of different faiths meeting to have a conversation. But the character of the conversation and the purpose of having the conversation are not simple to describe or categorize since they cover a variety of types. Leonard Swidler describes interfaith dialogue as a conversation among people of different faiths on a common subject, the primary purpose of which is for each participant to learn from the other so that he or she can change and grow: "But dialogue is *not* debate. In dialogue each partner must listen to the other as openly and sympathetically as s/he can in an attempt to understand the other's position as precisely and, as it were, as much from within, as possible. Such an attitude automatically includes the assumption that at any point we might find the partner's position so persuasive that . . . we would have to change."6 Swidler asserts that interreligious dialogue operates in three areas: "the practical, where we collaborate to help humanity; the depth or 'spiritual' dimension, where we attempt to experience the partner's religion or ideology 'from within'; the cognitive, where we seek understanding [of] the truth."7

When interfaith dialogue is used to contribute to international peacebuilding—the focus of this book—the emphasis is on the first of Swidler's categories, helping humanity. But experiencing the partner's religion can contribute to the peacebuilding process as well. Interfaith dialogue is often practiced in situations of peace because there are issues even in a peaceful context that can helpfully be addressed. Prejudice by members of one religious community toward those of another and religious discrimination toward members of religious minorities can be subjects of dialogue, as can other issues that generate tension, such as one religious community proselytizing and seeking converts within another religious community. Even more urgent is interfaith dialogue in situations of armed conflict, particularly when religion is one of the sources of conflict or when those in conflict are differentiated by religious identity. Most of the cases included in this book are of this kind.

Diana Eck asserts that interfaith dialogue can be the basis for the creation of one world. "One world cannot be built on the foundation of competition and polarization between the superpowers. One world cannot be built on the foundation of science, technology and the media. One world cannot be built on Christian, Muslim, Jewish or Sikh triumphalism. One world cannot be built on the foundation of mutual fear and suspicion.... Laying the foundations for one world is the most important task of our time. These foundations are not negotiated statements and agreements. These foundations are, rather, in the stockpiling of trust through dialogue and the creation of relationships that can sustain both agreements and disagreements."[8]

Based on his experience in the Balkans, Paul Mojzes states that "one could argue that religious leaders are able to find inspiration in their holy scripture and other traditions and writings to work with one another even when the relationship between politicians and the population is strained to the utmost and distrust prevails in society." He goes on to note that in situations of armed conflict it is a mistake to wait for the conflict to end before interreligious dialogue is initiated.[9] In calling for Muslims to join with Jews and Christians in "the frustrating and exhilarating process of dialogue," Israeli author Yossi Klein Halevi describes interfaith dialogue as "the true spiritual adventure of our time."[10]

Dialogue sessions that do not have a clearly defined purpose are almost inevitably doomed to ineffectiveness. Targeted dialogue can take a variety of forms and serve a variety of purposes, including these:

◆ High-level religious leaders can be convened to speak collectively as advocates for peace. The focus is joint action on behalf of peace. This can be particularly effective where religious divisions are among the sources of societal division and conflict. R. Scott Appleby has termed this approach the "elite leadership model."[11]

◆ Elite interfaith bodies can also engage in mediation between combatants to try to reach peace agreements, as was the case with the Interreligious Council of Sierra Leone and a comparable group in northern Uganda. These efforts are often most effective when they employ religious precepts and rituals in the mediation process.

◆ At the other extreme are grassroots efforts that bring participants together across religious divisions to provide a mechanism for cross-community dialogue and to nurture the development of participants into agents of reconciliation. Such forums often provide opportunities for sharing grievances and articulating the suffering of communities in conflict.[12] These sessions may also identify the peacebuilding resources inherent within each faith tradition. A variation on this approach focuses on transforming relationships among participants, often with an emphasis on prayer and repentance for sins committed. The admission of guilt by members of one group for past wrongs committed against the other religious group can provide a powerful basis for healing.

◆ Another approach is to highlight the theological and scriptural similarities among religious groups in conflict, as well as to seek to ameliorate the hostility that may be engendered by theological differences. A variation on this approach is for groups of different faiths to jointly study the sacred texts of each religion as a means to deepen understanding of one another's beliefs. Similarly, interfaith groups can share their religious rituals to enhance mutual understanding.

◆ Dialogue can be organized while conflict is ongoing, as a step toward ending the conflict, or in the postconflict period, as a contribution toward reconciliation.

◆ Training in conflict resolution for an interreligious group can serve as a vehicle for interfaith dialogue.

◆ Some writers note the severe limitations of dialogue that is confined to words and talk. They argue that deeds of reconciliation, particularly shared deeds among enemies, reaching across religious boundaries, are usually much more effective than merely engaging in interreligious conversation.

The main assertion of this book is that interfaith dialogue can be used as an effective tool to advance peacebuilding, but anyone who has engaged in interfaith dialogue in situations of serious conflict recognizes how difficult it is to organize and conduct meaningful interfaith dialogue. The fact that we have encountered many instances of interfaith sessions degenerating into shouting matches has prompted the writing of this book with recommendations on how to make interfaith sessions productive. Participants may not even approach the process with a deep knowledge of the theology and history of their own faith community. More significant, they are likely to carry into the process a set of preconceptions and prejudices regarding the beliefs and practices of the other religious community in the dialogue. When differences in religious belief and practice generate differences in convictions about how a society should be structured, the potential obstacles to effective dialogue multiply. And when the two religious groups have been on opposite sides of an armed conflict, even when religion has not been the principal basis for conflict, participants confront a history of hostility, injuries inflicted, and varying combinations of anger, hatred, and guilt that seriously compound the complexity of the dialogue process. If participants are expected to move beyond the past to joint planning for the future, the process is further complicated.

The experiences related in this book are largely confined to those orchestrated by U.S.-based organizations. This reflects the mandate of the United States Institute of Peace rather than a belief that the best interfaith dialogue has its origins in the United States. A great deal of creative work in this field is undertaken by organizations based outside the United States. The purpose of the Institute's Religion and Peacemaking Initiative is to assist religious organizations based in the United States to become more effective international peacemakers. This book has been conceived as one means of contributing to that end, hence the focus on U.S. organizations.

The fact that this book focuses exclusively on interfaith dialogue does not imply that interfaith dialogue is the only means by which religious organizations can contribute to peace. Faith-based nongovernmental organizations (NGOs) and other religious organizations very effectively contribute to peace through conducting training on conflict resolution, mediating between parties in conflict, engaging in conflict prevention, promoting nonviolent methodologies, organizing postcoflict reconciliation, and devising various other approaches to conflict resolution as part of their relief and development programs.[13]

Interfaith dialogue is thus an important but not the sole strategy that religious organizations can employ to advance peace.

The chapters in this book are divided into three parts. The first three chapters provide broad analytic assessments of interfaith dialogue, including its limitations. Mohammed Abu-Nimer, building primarily on his experience in the Middle East, focuses on the unique features of interfaith dialogue as opposed to other peacebuilding strategies. He also assesses the various types of interfaith dialogue and sets out some of the requirements for effective interfaith sessions. Marc Gopin focuses on the limitations of dialogue that is confined to talk. He argues for the shared study of sacred texts and symbolic acts of apology, undertaken on a reciprocal basis. Jaco Cilliers draws from his experience in places such as South Africa, Bosnia, and the Philippines and asserts that dialogue must address the justice issues that underlie the conflict.

Part II consists of three case studies in specific zones of conflict. Ronald Young discusses dialogue on the Middle East among American Jews, Christians, and Muslims. He points out that the dialogue process forces Christians, Jews, and Muslims to confront some of their deepest fears and most persistent prejudices about one another. David Steele relates his experiences in Bosnia, Serbia, Croatia, and Kosovo. He asserts the value of dialogue among the middle ranges of religious leadership, engaging both clergy and lay leaders. Through his efforts to organize postwar reconciliation in the Balkans he has concluded that storytelling and the mutual admission of sin committed during the conflict have the greatest impact. Joseph Liechty addresses interfaith dialogue in Northern Ireland and advocates a methodology, which he terms mitigation, that can be used to ameliorate religious conflict when theological differences feed intergroup tensions.

Part III contains two chapters that analyze the experiences of particular organizations. Arthur Schneier discusses dialogues organized by the Appeal of Conscience Foundation, which follows the elite leadership model. In such places as the Balkans the foundation has convened religious leaders to issue joint declarations for peace and to institutionalize interreligious bodies. Charles Gibbs describes what has been learned by the United Religions Initiative in its dialogue work, convening interreligious cooperation circles whose purpose is deep spiritual sharing and the organization of joint projects, often peacemaking projects.

The concluding chapter draws together a number of lessons from the experiences presented in the preceding chapters, lessons that underscore the great potential of interfaith dialogue and suggest how it can be more effectively realized.

NOTES

1. Hans Küng, *Christianity and the World Religions: Paths of Dialogue with Islam, Hinduism, and Buddhism* (Garden City, N.Y.: Doubleday, 1986), 442.

2. "Never the Twain Shall Peacefully Meet?" *Economist,* November 17, 2001.

3. Thomas L. Friedman, "The Real War," *New York Times,* November 27, 2001, A21.

4. David Little et al., "Religion, World Order, and Peace" (paper presented at the Millennium World Peace Summit of Religious and Spiritual Leaders, New York, August 2000), 2.

5. Ibid., 4.

6. Leonard Swidler, *Theoria-Praxis: How Jews, Christians, and Muslims Can Together Move from Theory to Practice* (Leuven, Belgium: Uitgeverij Peeters, 1998), 24.

7. Ibid., 28.

8. Diana Eck, in *Minutes, Sixth Meeting of the Working Group of Dialogue with People of Living Faiths* (Geneva: World Council of Churches, 1985), 20–30.

9. Paul Mojzes, "The Role of Religious Leaders in Times of Conflict in Multinational and Multireligious Societies" (unpublished manuscripts, November 2001).

10. Yossi Klein Halevi, "A Coming Together We Must Take on Faith,"*Washington Post,* December 23, 2001, B3.

11. R. Scott Appleby, *The Ambivalence of the Sacred: Religion, Violence, and Reconciliation* (Lanham, Md.: Rowman and Littlefield, 2000), 223.

12. See ibid., 188.

13. See *Faith-Based NGOs and International Peacebuilding,* United States Institute of Peace Special Report (Washington, D.C.: United States Institute of Peace, October 22, 2001).

Part 1

Promises and Challenges
of Interfaith Dialogue

1

The Miracles of Transformation through Interfaith Dialogue

Are You a Believer?

Mohammed Abu-Nimer

*D*IALOGUE IS A VERY DANGEROUS BUSINESS," I have been told again and again by participants and observers of dialogue workshops and peacebuilding training. Once opponents meet in a genuine dialogue setting, they will never return to the same positions or level of awareness that they had before. It is as if they have joined a new society. Their views and perceptions of the conflict and the enemy change, mostly because of the powerful turning point in the dialogue process when participants realize, acknowledge, and understand their mutual fears and concerns. When that bridge is constructed between the two sides, a powerful connection has been made—one that separates dialoguers from nondialoguers. After the dialogue experience, participants report that they develop new and more sensitive radars for language of hatred, exclusion, and prejudice (Abu-Nimer 1999). Others become deeply involved in actions to improve the conditions of their communities. Dialoguing with the enemy has its price, too. One of the obstacles facing dialoguers is the accusation that they are giving up the fight against injustice. But the opposite is true. Dialogue is not a substitute for social action. Protest and resistance to oppression are still needed for social and political change to occur. However, dialogue provides an additional path on which to accomplish such changes. It is a path that is full of positive and constructive joint energy and that is based on creativity and trust.

During the 1990s there was a sharp rise in the amount of research in and practice of interreligious peacebuilding (see Abu-Nimer 1996; Assefa 1993; Curle 1990; Johansen 1997; Johnston and Sampson 1994; Kasimow and Byron 1991; and Smock 1998). Scholars and practitioners are becoming increasingly interested in exploring the potential impact of religion as a source of peacemaking rather than discussing it as a source of violence and war.[1] In conflict areas, various nongovernmental organizations are initiating interfaith training and dialogue workshops to promote peacebuilding from a religious perspective rather than from the typical focus on interethnic relations.

Is the interfaith dialogue process different from a secular or nonreligious (interethnic or intercultural) dialogue process? How do the features of interfaith dialogue influence the potential outcomes of the dialogue process? What are the shortcomings of traditional approaches to promoting productive interfaith interaction, and what new approaches are likely to be more effective? Indeed, many participants in interreligious training workshops in peacebuilding are puzzled when asked to explain the difference between interfaith dialogue and a secular or nonreligious dialogue. Therefore, it is important to identify the unique features of interfaith dialogue and to compare them to those of nonreligious or nonfaith-based dialogue.[2]

WHY AN INTERFAITH APPROACH?

Spirituality

Spirituality is at the center of the interfaith encounter and is the most powerful feature of interfaith dialogue because it allows change in participants' attitudes. Three elements have been identified in typical interethnic dialogue and training groups that are necessary for achieving and maintaining positive change in participants' attitudes to the "other": (1) alternative cognitive processes through new information and analysis (change in the head), (2) a positive emotional experience in meeting the other through the construction of a safe and trusting relationship (change in the heart), and (3) working together on a concrete task or action that enforces the positive attitudinal change (change through the hand) (Abu-Nimer 2001a).

When employing the above elements in interfaith dialogue or training, participants often utilize their spiritual identities (beliefs and values) to pursue transformation or change in their perceptions of a conflict. In the change that occurs through spiritual framework, dialoguers not only receive new information, have a positive emotional experience, or accomplish a joint project, but also make a deeper human connection with each other through their spiritual encounter. When this "deeper spiritual connection" is made in the interfaith dialogue, it becomes the main source for the individual's commitment to social change, peace work, and taking the risks to confront one's own evil.[3]

This deep sense of motivation that originates from religious identity distinguishes interfaith dialogue from secular or interethnic encounter. When asked what is unique about interfaith dialogue, participants in one interreligious peacebuilding training offered the following comments:

> "Religion touches upon deeper levels of our identity."
>
> "We become more sensitive and attentive when it comes to our religious identity."
>
> "Religious feelings can mobilize people faster than any other elements of their identity."
>
> "There is no risk that I will lose my religion if I meet people from the other religion."
>
> "Moral and spiritual forces of religion can encourage people to act and change."
>
> "If participants change their attitudes in interfaith dialogue, such change will be deeper than if the change occurred in a nonreligious context."

The depth of religious experience can surface quickly in interreligious interaction. For example, in a discussion between Muslims and Christians from Europe and North America on their current relationship, the Muslim participants quickly raised the issue of the eleventh-century

Crusades, opining that the deep-seated mistrust between Muslims and Christians originated during that period. Most Christian participants were unaware that such historic events constituted a significant factor in the collective memory of today's Muslims.

Thus, religious identity in dialogue can be a source of powerful change owing to the deep convictions that bind participants to their particular religion. However, such deep convictions can be a source of resistance to change, too.

Rituals

The use of and the emphasis on rituals and symbols also set interfaith dialogue apart from interethnic dialogue. The use and the extent of rituals vary in every religion; however, rituals are powerful means of communication among members of the same religion. Through them, followers of a religion connect to their spiritual sources and observe their values and beliefs. In interfaith dialogue, rituals create a mode of dialogue. Understanding another religion's rituals opens a window onto the meaning system of the other. Participating in another's rituals allows members of the interfaith dialogue group to temporarily experience the other's worldview. Obviously, participants should carefully consider the types of rituals that all members of the interfaith group can experience together. Some rituals may offend the other or contradict the other's beliefs. For example, it may be more awkward for a Muslim to take part in a Christian communion than it may be for a Christian to fast with a Muslim one day during Ramadan or to remember those who have died on the morning of the Al Fitr and Al Adha feasts.[4]

Dialogue groups often create their own rituals and symbols through the dialogue process to celebrate a "third culture." Participants tend to derive such rituals and symbols from their traditions. Because they hold spiritual meaning, these new rituals and symbols often lead the group to a deeper level of dialogue. For instance, participants in one training workshop brought in items from their religion and culture and offered them to the group as a collective gift. After a few offerings, the group arranged them in the middle of the room, declaring it an offering site to the human spirit of peace. When all members completed their gift sharing, the center of the room looked like a holy site where members of a faith had offered gifts and sacrifices to their god.[5] Such exercises in interethnic dialogue groups cannot achieve this level of meaning or interpretation. The spiritual practices and the religious identity of the participants in interfaith dialogue allow rituals to have deeper meaning in group interaction.[6]

Scripture and Sacred Texts

Scripture and sacred texts enrich interfaith dialogue. Participants can default or turn to studying or interpreting their sacred books when they feel that other avenues of dialogue are not getting them anywhere or that the dialogue process is too risky. For instance, a group of Muslim, Christian, and Jewish dialoguers constructed initial meetings to share readings from their holy books that related to certain themes (land, Jerusalem, peace, and so on). The reading and interpretation process served as a safe mechanism for learning about one another's religious interpretations and avoiding a direct political debate over these issues.

Scripture and sacred texts provide a level of "certainty" and "truth" to interfaith dialoguers. Thus it is a painful experience when the dialogue process leads some participants to complete uncertainty and causes them to question their basic values and perceptions. However, in many cases, scripture and sacred texts can function as a foundation, providing faithful participants with direction and confidence during the process of demythologization and discovery. For example, a Filipino Muslim participant constantly referred to his holy book, the Qur'an, when he gained insight after interacting with Filipino Christians. His deep belief in the holy book helped him cope with breaking the illusions and myths that he had held regarding Catholics. Several Catholic priests and nuns reported similar experiences during their dialogue process. Muslims helped the priests and nuns become aware of the stereotypical images, prejudices, and social and historical injustices they had of the Moro (members of the Muslim minority in the Philippines) and indigenous people. One Catholic priest illustrated this transformation when he pulled out his sacred text and said, "The Bible instructs us to be open to change, and to accept and recognize our weakness. We all have prejudice."[7]

Secondary and Universal Language of Peace
versus Primary Language

Politics is an explosive topic in interethnic dialogue. When participants engage in political debate, particularly in the early stage of the process, they mobilize their defense mechanisms and fortify and harden their stereotypical attitudes toward and prejudices of the other. In interfaith dialogue, primary language and particular religious rituals can also provoke defensiveness if used early in the process. For example, in the first day of an encounter, Muslims became annoyed and defensive when Christians began talking about the Holy Trinity.[8] Similarly, when Muslims declared that infidels are those who do not believe in one god or who worship multiple gods, Hindus and Buddhists in the group expressed their discomfort and inability to dialogue with the Muslims. There are certain risks when participants use their primary language (that is, beliefs and terms that are unique to a faith group and often not used by others) without much prior warning or preparation. This type of language may contain certain contradictions with others' religious beliefs and therefore makes the others uncomfortable and causes them to compete by using their own primary language.

A Middle Eastern Christian priest eager to share his passion for peace and harmony offered to start the morning reflection of a diverse religious group with a song. The group included at least twelve different denominations and religions. He asked all the participants to repeat the words to a song calling for the praise and joy of Jesus the Lord. The group seemed uncomfortable with the song, but many repeated the words, others hummed, and a few remained silent. When asked about their reaction, an Afghani Muslim woman said, "It was difficult at the beginning, but then I replaced Jesus with Muhammad and I felt no problem with the song after that."

Such reactions or dynamics often indicate that dialoguers have little tolerance for other religious narratives. To avoid such sentiment, most experienced interfaith dialoguers begin by using universal or religious secondary language to emphasize the virtues and ideals they share with others. For example, they discuss peace, love, harmony, charity, devotion to their beliefs, doing good, and so forth in a language everyone can understand and to which everyone can relate.

Secondary language helps participants discover their similarities and creates an atmosphere of trust that encourages meaningful interaction. Secondary language gets participants moving toward the process of exploring religious differences as well as political positions.

Similar processes can take place in interethnic or secular dialogue. However, to acknowledge similarities in such dialogue, participants must explore their cultural and personal norms and values. They emphasize their desire for peace. However, the uniqueness of the interfaith dialogue is that every religion more or less possesses a universal secondary language that can bridge the gap between participants and provide them with a vernacular with which to explore their differences at a later stage.

BASIC PRINCIPLES OF EFFECTIVE INTERFAITH DIALOGUE

In dialogue groups, certain conditions can contribute to the success of the encounter (Abu-Nimer 1999; Saunders 1999). The following guidelines are not necessarily unique to an effective interfaith dialogue process; they certainly apply to interethnic context as well.

Symmetric Arrangements in the Process and Design

Addressing the imbalance of power that exists outside the dialogue room (or in reality) is central in designing and managing an effective interfaith dialogue process. For instance, when Palestinian Muslims and Christians meet with Israeli Jews, the realities of the conflict impose different power relations. Jewish authorities control Muslim holy sites and property and Christian churches and clergy are under constant Israeli surveillance, while Jewish religious sites, rituals, and so on are protected and well represented in the culture. The interfaith dialogue framework cannot bring such imbalance of power into the dialogue without intentionally addressing it through various arrangements (changes in the locations, timing, setup, and so on). A better balance of power can be achieved, for example, by providing security (often the mere location of the dialogue threatens certain members of the group) for participants or by choosing a site that is not necessarily associated with Jewish culture or religion.

Selection of Appropriate Participants

Participants' commitment, qualifications, and background are crucial to the success of any dialogue process. When selecting clergy and religious participants, organizers ought to pay special attention to the qualifications and credentials of the invitees. When inviting rabbis who are well educated and familiar with their religious texts and well versed in their religious sources, organizers should make sure that the Muslim and Christian clergy are also well educated and familiar with their religious texts and sources. If conveners do not seek such balance among invitees, they may perpetuate the power imbalance that exists outside the dialogue group. Another way to balance power is to ensure that the dialogue is co-led or co-facilitated by each of the religious groups rather than to have a member of the majority religion convene as well as lead the interfaith dialogue. For example, in most of the interfaith dialogue groups in Israel, the convener is Jewish, while the Muslim and Christian invitees symbolically share the stage. In fact, interfaith organizations in Israel are often led by Jewish directors, while Muslims and Christians are either board members or just participants. Effective interfaith dialogue cannot serve the interests of only the majority.

Examination of Both Similarities and Differences

Religious differences, like ethnic and national differences, are usually perceived as threatening to the harmony of the dialogue groups. Thus, many dialoguers prefer to touch on or explore the similarities and unique practices of each religion or religious culture. For example, if some groups are interested in Muslim rituals, practices, and beliefs, they would focus on the unique aspects of the Ramadan fasting, the principles of *zakat* (almsgiving), and similarities between the stories of Joseph, Moses, and Jesus told in the Qur'an and the stories told in the Bible. Interfaith dialogue groups can spend months or years exploring similarities in their practices and celebrating their unique rituals and shared emphases on peace, love, understanding, and tolerance. In other words, the group can remain at the secondary-language conversation level. Most Jewish, Muslim, and Christian dialogue groups initially emphasize the secondary language of humanism and universalism in each faith. Participants are quick to declare with pride that their religion is one of peace and harmony. Such emphasis on similarities is a necessary condition or step for building trust and for discovering the human bond that ties Jews, Muslims, and Christians as people of faith. However, if this approach becomes the main theme of the interfaith dialogue and is used to avoid dealing with inherent religious differences, then the dialogue creates an artificial harmony—one that does not convey the complexity of the inherent interreligious contradictions and differences among Judaism, Christianity, and Islam.

Interfaith dialogue should work to offset core differences among faith groups and deal with values and beliefs that may justify exclusion of and prejudice against other people. For instance, interreligious dialogue among Muslims, Jews, and Christians has to explore their different interpretations and understandings of such values and beliefs as the Holy Trinity, jihad, absolute justice, and Chosen People. Realizing the implications of such beliefs on the interreligious reality in Israel/Palestine is a significant outcome of the dialogue process. Appreciating interreligious differences can lead the members to identify their different interpretations and understand—and even critically evaluate—their religious belief system.

Inclusion of a Collaborative Task

Through the dialogue forums, participants gain important insights into the other's religion and develop empathy for the other's beliefs and religious practices. But is this sufficient for a successful interfaith dialogue group? For the religious majority, insight and empathy may often be sufficient. But members of the religious minority tend to demand more than "talk" and "insights." Actions and concrete results were the terms used by Muslims and Christian Palestinians when they engaged in dialogue with Jews. They often asked, "What will this produce?" and "Where does it lead us?" in the first meeting or when invited to participate.

Again, to address the power imbalance in reality and to be sensitive to the needs of the religious minority, it is important to incorporate an action or collaborative task that members of the interfaith dialogue group can select or negotiate (for example, building a classroom, funding a youth club, sponsoring a multireligious class, participating in a protest). When interfaith meetings were initiated in southern Egypt following the bloody clashes between Muslims and Christians in 1996, development projects were the bridge that helped participants meet and restore some order in their communities.[9] Agricultural projects funded by European organizations were used to create joint meetings between Christians and Muslims in the various villages.

In addition to empowering the religious minority, a collaboration such as a concrete development project allows members to interact safely and default to an action or a task when their ideological or theological differences are at an impasse. Also, the successful outcome of any concrete project will contribute to the development of minority communities and will provide minority participants with much-needed credibility and support for their efforts to engage in or attend an interfaith dialogue forum.

Flexible Process of Interaction

As in other dialogue forums, flexibility in the interaction process is highly important for an effective interaction (Saunders 1999). A flexible process in interfaith dialogue means that conveners and facilitators are not locked into one model or structure of practice. The developments and spiraling dynamics of the conflict in which interreligious dialogue takes place are part of the reality. Members of the interreligious dialogue group need to present to their communities constructive ways to handle the constant destructive conflict developments. To do that, the process and design need to be flexible and tuned to reality. A multicast group that meets in Israel and focuses its entire work on studying the scriptures, with little or no deliberate attention to the dozens of people who are being killed and injured every day, is detached from reality. Praying for the victims on both sides is a political act that may remove participants from the objective of reading and focusing on attaining a deeper understanding of their scriptures, but it is more connected to the surrounding reality and may engage hundreds of other people in the dialogue efforts.

For example, in July and August 2001, hundreds of Palestinians and tens of Israelis were killed in a massive escalation of violence. In such situations, interfaith dialogue groups cannot interact in the way they normally do. They have to be creative and flexible to generate interaction and activity that allow them to be constructive and avoid being swept away by the rush of violence. Reading from Jewish, Islamic, and Christian scriptures may be one activity, but it takes many other initiatives to bring a different voice to this spiral of conflict.

Healing and Acknowledgment of Collective and Individual Injuries

Dialogue is a powerful tool that deepens individuals' understanding of the other's perspectives and worldviews. One transformative phase occurs when members of conflicting groups mutually acknowledge their side's collective wrongdoing against the other. Such acknowledgment takes place when there is enough security and trust in the group to walk through the parties' history and critically examine each side's responsibility in creating such history. In interfaith dialogue, religious sources for peace become powerful tools to help the group engage in the process of "walking through the history" and acknowledging collective wrongdoing. Rituals of forgiveness and healing can set participants on the path to reconciliation. Activities from different religious traditions can be used for "meeting the other" and enriching the perspective of all participants (Henderson 1996).

For example, Palestinian Muslims and Christians and Israeli Jews can examine their history through religious lenses by responding to the question, When and how were your religious values of peace, tolerance, and protection of human life violated by your religious group? Another example of collective acknowledgment is a deep examination of the concepts of forgiveness and healing among the different traditions.[10] The three traditions in the Middle East—Judaism, Christianity, and Islam—have rich cultural and religious sources to engage their followers in the process of healing and forgiveness.[11]

Unireligious Preparation and Forums

Prior to any organized dialogue, it is essential to conduct a series of separate meetings in which members of each faith (1) explore their stand on the controversial issues, (2) establish both unity and diversity within their own group, (3) discuss and choose methods for their interfaith dialogue experience, and (4) set the collective and individual criteria for a success-ful interfaith dialogue.

Having such a unireligious meeting before the interfaith dialogue ensures that members of each religious group understand and appreciate the differences and similarities in their collective religious experience. It provides support to members who feel or know that they are taking a high risk by attending an interfaith dialogue encounter or training. In addition, the intrareligious meetings enhance the members' knowledge and awareness of the various levels of understanding within their own religious group. It is crucial to recognize that unireligious peace meetings are appropriate and can be even more effective than interfaith dialogue. A rabbis' group that does not often meet with Palestinian Muslims or Christians for dialogue but nonetheless advocates for human rights in the occupied territories may affect more religious and secular Jews than an interfaith group that meets regularly to deepen its understanding of other religions. A Christian or Muslim organization that operates among the Palestinians and educates for tolerance and peaceful negotiation may affect Palestinian opinion more than those religious organizations that rush to conduct joint activities. Similarly, a religious Jewish-based group that operates in the United States to promote a message of peace in Israel through public media and other activities can have more influence on the U.S. Jewish community than an interfaith group of Jews, Muslims, and Christians that also operates in the United States.[12] Such a strategy is particularly important when the communities are trapped in a violent cycle that often prevents joint activities.

A PROCESS OF INTERFAITH DIALOGUE

Like any forum for dialogue, the interfaith forum is effective when it is designed and managed to provide measures of safety while participants discover each other's similarities and differences. When participants are threatened, uncomfortable, or unready to explore differences, they fall back on their preconceived notions and stereotypes of the other. In addition, any form of learning new information and skills requires people to take a certain degree of risk and to abandon or suspend their existing knowledge and attitudes toward the other. It is the duty of the facilitators and designers of the interfaith dialogue to ensure that the atmosphere encourages participants to take the required risk to learn and act.

Obviously, any dialogue process is not linear and its phases cannot be mechanically separated. There are too many factors that influence the outcomes and dynamics of each interfaith dialogue. Thus, it is impossible to identify or list all of them. However, there are four phases of development in an effective experiment in interfaith dialogue. These phases can be incorporated into different settings; however, the following order tends to capture many of the Muslim, Christian, and Jewish interfaith dialogue group dynamics. Some groups may remain for years in the first and second phases. In fact, one interfaith group has been created to avoid political differences and religious tension. The group focuses its mission on discovering similarities and emphasizing religious harmony. Other interfaith groups incorporate elements from the third and fourth phases as early as the second meeting. Some of the factors that influence such dynamics are (1) experience of participants and conveners in such settings, (2) level of awareness among facilitators and participants of the power dynamics in their conflict realities, (3) degree of imbalance of power among participants and conveners, and (4) funding stipulations and agencies.[13]

Phase One

In the first phase, participants express their excitement at meeting members of other religions. They engage in a series of activities and dynamics that reflect the tension, joy, politeness, and kindness experienced when meeting the others. In this phase, the focus is on exploring individual and group similarities. Also, most participants engage in a form of idealization of their own religion. Muslim participants are always quick to point out that in Arabic the word *Islam* is derived from *salaam*, which means peace. Many Jewish participants point out their ancient roots and preservation of their faith throughout history. Christians in a typical Middle Eastern fashion emphasize their belief in forgiveness and healing.

Phase Two

In the second phase, religious and cultural tension and caution persist, but participants begin to learn more about the differences among the groups.

The personal, cultural, and religious acquaintance process continues; however, more emphasis is placed on similarities among religions. During this phase, participants reveal personal stereotypes about other religions. The setting becomes less threatening because of the intensive informal contacts and the discovery of the universal rituals and ceremonies that connect participants. This environment is reflected through the use of secondary religious language (peace, love, harmony, faith, brotherhood, sacrifice) as each religion expresses it. In this process of discovering religious similarities, dialoguers tend to create joint rituals or ceremonies that allow them to practice their faiths separately but beside each other, for example, using secondary language from the Bible and Qur'an in a joint prayer.

Phase Three

Throughout the third phase, participants explore different religious beliefs and values. The realization of differences can cause frustration, mistrust, suspicion, blame, and tension, the level of which depends on the relationship (mainly the level of trust and personal links) that has developed among the different religious groups and individuals in the encounter. It is in this stage that participants address questions such as, What are the major contradicting beliefs and practices in our religions? What beliefs and practices in each religion exclude the others? Muslim and Jewish participants usually express the highest level of tension in encounters during this phase. Beliefs such as jihad, Chosen People, and no salvation outside the church are discussed and reinterpreted or explained. At the end of this stage, participants discover and confirm the differences in religious values and faith practices. Many participants repeat statements regarding the importance of interreligious tolerance to ensure the legitimacy of differences and to emphasize the principle of tolerating differences.

Phase Four

By the fourth phase, participants have recognized the limits and advantages of interreligious peacebuilding encounters. They feel empowered because of their ability to connect to other religions and their new understanding of peacebuilding in their own religion. Most participants have become more trusting of and less threatened by other religions. They emphasize the agreements, restate similarities, and define the sensitive issues. In this phase, participants can explore alternatives to interreligious competition and violence. They search for common activities or practical applications for their agreements and apply their improved ability to learn and understand the other religions. This stage of the interreligious dialogue emphasizes action. Participants develop a specific, concrete, and feasible action plan to apply on returning to their communities. Also, participants can identify the resources for religious peacebuilding in their own communities and others. As part of this phase, participants can start mapping the landscape of the interreligious organizations at the national and international levels.

CONCLUSION

Religious identity is one of the most powerful sources in shaping attitudes and actions in a conflict zone. The observant and the non-observant are quick to accept death and violence in the name of their religion. It is only recently that scholars and practitioners have begun systematically exploring how to use people's strong and deep religious identity or affiliation in the processes of peacebuilding. Interfaith dialogue is only one of the methods by which peacebuilders can use religion to change certain conflict settings.

An interreligious dialogue or encounter is similar to dialogue initiatives carried out in a secular (interethnic) context. However, certain unique features in an interfaith dialogue setting require content and process designs that differ from those in a typical secular setting. The spiritual, moral, and ethical components of any religious identity are powerful sources for generating change.

NOTES

1. Some of these studies (such as Appleby 1998; Gopin 2000; and Johnston and Sampson 1994) deal with general and comparative research on peacebuilding in different traditions. Others (including Said, Funk, and Kadayifci 2001; Abu-Nimer 2002; Lederach 2000; Sachedina 2001; and Smock 1998) focus on religious sources of peace in one tradition.

2. This article is based on reactions of participants in three peacebuilding training groups that discussed interreligious peacebuilding during the summer of 2001. One hundred sixty people participated in four programs: the Summer Peacebuilding Institute (SPI) at Eastern Mennonite University, in Harrisonburg, Virginia; the Contact Summer Program at the School of International Training (SIT) in Vermont; the Mindanao Peacebuilding Institute (MPI) in Davao City, the Philippines; and the Summer Peacebuilding and Development Institute at American University in Washington, D.C.

3. Gordon and Gordon (1991) suggest that, in dialogue, participants learn to confront the evil forces in their own community.

4. Muslims visit the graves of their relatives and members of the community in the early morning of every *eid* (feast day). In many Muslim communities, after the prayer on the grave, the family offers sweets to those who join them.

5. The same process of creating a shared sacred site with members' religious and cultural symbols took place among thirty-eight participants from eight different religious groups at SPI in Virginia and among thirty-two participants from seven religious groups at MPI in the Philippines (these groups included Catholics, Muslims, Quakers, Mennonites, Greek Orthodox, Protestants, Jews, Hindus, Buddhists, and Sufis).

6. Based on peacebuilding training conducted at SIT, summer 2001.

7. MPI, June 2001.

8. Muslim participants rejected the belief that Jesus is the son of God.

9. SPI, June 9, 1999, an interview with an Egyptian Coptic priest who assisted in launching one such development project.

10. In June 2001, the Israel Interfaith Association organized a panel discussion on the meaning of *shahid* (martyr) in Judaism, Christianity, and Islam. A Muslim sheik, a Jewish rabbi, and a Christian priest explored the different meanings of this concept in the three traditions ("The Meaning of Martyr/'Shahid' in World Religions," *Israel Interfaith Association Newsletter* [June 2001]). Religious rituals have been used to begin the lengthy processes of healing in other conflicts, too. In Rwanda, the Catholic Church, in its efforts to deal with the genocide, re-baptized many priests in one of the rivers to symbolize a new beginning and healing (peacebuilding workshop in Sierra Leone, 1997, sponsored by CARE, U.S.A.).

11. See Marc Gopin, "Forgiveness as an Element of Conflict Resolution in Religious Cultures: Walking the Tightrope of Reconciliation and Justice," in Abu-Nimer 2001b.

12. Since early 2001, some Jewish and Christian groups in Washington, D.C., (and nationally) have been working separately to organize a campaign to stop the violence in Israel/Palestine and to assist the two sides in restarting their peace negotiations. They are also working to put public pressure on the U.S. government to intervene directly and end its "hands-off" policy. (Mubarak Awad of

Nonviolence International, and Kathy Bergen of American Friends Committee, conversations with author on June 3, 2001, and May 31, 2001, respectively.)

13. For further discussion on the conditions for effective encounter, see Abu-Nimer 1999; and Hewstone and Brown 1986.

REFERENCES

Abu-Nimer, Mohammed. 1996. "Conflict Resolution and Islam: Some Conceptual Questions." *Peace and Change* 21 (January): 22–40.

———. 1999. *Dialogue, Conflict Resolution, and Change: Arab-Jewish Encounters in Israel.* Albany, N.Y.: State University of New York Press.

———. 2001a. "Conflict Resolution and Religion: Toward a Training Model of Interreligious Peacebuilding." *Journal of Peace Research* 38, no. 6 (November).

———. 2001b. *Reconciliation, Justice, and Coexistence: Theory and Practice.* Lanham, Md.: Lexington Books.

———. 2002. *Nonviolence and Peacebuilding in Islamic Communities.* Gainesville: University Press of Florida. Forthcoming.

Appleby, Scott. 1998. *The Ambivalence of the Sacred: Religion, Violence, and Reconciliation.* New York: Rowman and Littlefield.

Assefa, Hizkias. 1993. *Peace and Reconciliation as a Paradigm.* Nairobi: Nairobi Peace Initiative.

Curle, Adam. 1990. *Tools for Transformation: A Personal Study.* Stroud, U.K.: Hawthorn Press.

Gopin, Marc. 2000. *Between Eden and Armageddon: The Future of World Religions, Violence, and Peacemaking.* New York: Oxford University Press.

Gordon, Haim, and Rivca Gordon, eds. 1991. *Israel/Palestine: The Quest for Dialogue.* New York: Orbis Books.

Henderson, Michael. 1996. *The Forgiveness Factor.* London: Grosvenor Books.

Hewstone, Miles, and Rupert Brown, eds. 1986. *Contact and Conflict in Intergroup Encounters.* Oxford: Basil Blackwell.

Johansen, Robert. 1997. "Radical Islam and Non-Violence: A Case Study of Religious Empowerment and Constraint among Pashtuns." *Journal of Peace Research* 34, no. 1: 53–71.

Johnston, Douglas, and Cynthia Sampson, eds. 1994. *Religion: The Missing Dimension of Statecraft.* New York: Oxford University Press.

Kasimow, Harold, and Sherwin Byron. 1991. *No Religion Is an Island: Abraham Joshua Heschel and Interreligious Dialogue.* New York: Maryknoll, 1991.

Lederach, John Paul. 2000. *The Journey toward Reconciliation.* Scottdale, Pa.: Herald Press.

Sachedina, Abdulaziz. 2001. *The Islamic Roots of Democratic Pluralism.* New York: Oxford University Press.

Said, Abdul Aziz, Nathan C. Funk, and Ayse S. Kadayifci, eds. 2001. *Peace and Conflict Resolution in Islam: Precept and Practice.* Lanham, Md.: University Press of America.

Saunders, Harold. 1999. *A Public Peace Process: Sustained Dialogue to Transform Racial and Ethnic Conflicts.* New York: St. Martin's Press.

Smock, David, ed. 1998. *Private Peacemaking: USIP-Assisted Peacemaking Projects of Non-Profit Organizations.* United States Institute of Peace Special Report. Washington, D.C.: United States Institute of Peace.

2

The Use of the Word and Its Limits

A Critical Evaluation of Religious Dialogue as Peacemaking

Marc Gopin

HE USE OF THE WORD as the principal means of peacemaking is ubiquitous in Western culture, at least among those who consider themselves peacemakers and diplomats. This is fundamentally flawed as far as an accurate picture of how, in fact, human beings reconcile and make peace, when they manage to do so.

Neither in practice nor in principle do words open us up to the vast range of possibilities in terms of how human beings change internally or how they transform their relationships externally with adversaries. Western cultures and, in parallel form, Abrahamic religions of the West, tend to be wordy and textual, or believe themselves to be. They tend to overemphasize the power of the word over the power of the deed, even though deed and ritual are actually deeply embedded in these religions. When it comes to peacemaking, the word becomes ubiquitous. We must analyze what religions have done till now with regard to the use of the word and then make recommendations for the future.

This should not be misunderstood as a broadside against any use of the word. Nothing is categorical here, but rather inclusive. It is an argument for what is missing, not an either/or formula. Furthermore, the use of the word is indispensable in all peacemaking when we come to the stage of negotiations, that is, once people find themselves willing and ready to come to the table in order to outline their differences and to agree on future arrangements.

There are subsets of the use of the word that include, for example, the use of the word for a written treaty, the use of the word in the context of dialogue, and the use of the word for study and training in conflict resolution. Dialogue is considered often to be the main or only means of conflict resolution. Many people use "dialogue" as the equivalent of "peacemaking" and "conflict resolution." But this is a mistake.

Family conflict, intercultural conflict, and international conflict are closely related for a variety of reasons that I will not go into here. But allow me to engage in a family conflict analogy for a moment. Whenever we have a dispute with our very verbal four-year-old we remind her to use her words, especially when she is very upset and starts to throw things or whine and cry. The truth is that, to the degree that one can get either enemies or four-year-olds to use their words, one will move closer to peace and away from confrontation. But one cannot always rely on this. Most four-year-olds happen to be less articulate than my daughter at this stage, and even she has many moods that go well beyond what she is capable of articulating. Most of us do.

Most enemies cannot or will not articulate their true feelings through the use of words in dialogue. Either it is beyond their present capacity or what they really feel is too shameful. Examples of things too difficult to articulate may include deep envy, or shame at the collective humiliation of one's group, or an intense desire to humiliate, or to take revenge, or to see the enemy suffer.

This reluctance to articulate skews the words that do get used because they cloak much darker emotions at work. Furthermore, conducting a war is often considered far more virile and honorable than articulating in words the feelings of envy for an enemy group, and therefore dialogic peacemaking is seen as weakness and defeat.

Nevertheless, religious words are used in a variety of circumstances, some of which have the advantage of moving intense emotions of hatred into a different mode of interaction. Often rational words and exchange are too hard, but healing words can be exchanged. One such example involves words or deeds that express reconciliation, regret, and apology. In the final stages of conflict processes many progressive people in the West envision reconciliation and apology.

Here again, however, the child parallels are instructive as to the complications of the use of the word. What comes naturally to my daughter after she has hurt us in some way is to sidle up next to us, looking for physical affection, or, alternatively, she explicitly acts as if nothing is wrong, hoping to go back to the old and good arrangement. But we are the ones who train her in such situations, several times a day it seems, to use the word "sorry" before resuming good relations. She, however, naturally uses emotional acts, such as affection, to reconcile, or symbolic actions, such as a broad smile.

These symbolic acts embody my daughter's way of saying "I'm sorry." Which is superior, her nonverbal way or our verbal instructions? Are we training her for something superior, the use of the word for reconciliation, or are we ignoring her natural capacities for reconciliation and failing to work with her natural means of ending a state of anger?

This is a central crux of conflict resolution analysis that remains unresolved. On one level, whatever comes naturally to a child, or to a culture or one class of people, may be preferred because, in essence, it works for them. But this path is very difficult to discern once we reach the infinite complexity of human diversity in multicultural contexts and complex international struggles. Even a single children's classroom or a single workplace may bring together many different orientations to reconciliation. Making generalizations about method becomes essentially unknowable owing to the infinite diversity of reactions.

What becomes paramount, perhaps, is access to as wide a range of means of reconciliation as possible, which includes both the word and the deed. The maximum range is necessary because the infinite complexity of human encounter across genders, religions, races, and countries requires great elasticity of engagement. This means that we must pursue dialogue as reconciliation, but with great humility and elasticity, ready and willing to combine it with or supplant it with other modes of reconciliation, especially in terms of deed, symbol, and emotional communication.

Even with my four-year-old, elasticity of method is preferable. We should listen as carefully to the way she reconciles as we expect her to listen to us. Naturally she needs in our society to learn the power and importance of negotiation, reconciliation, and apology through the word, but we need to learn as well. Of course, we are the adults/teachers/models. But without our deferring completely to Rousseau's prejudice toward natural states, an accurate view of life acknowledges that children are our teachers also, because we have often become flawed as adults in our ability to truly listen to the other.

Missing the cues of how the adversary, the alienated other, is trying to engage us is a profoundly understudied phenomenon. It cuts to the heart of the persistence of many family and international conflicts. For example, if one party expects words and the other expects emotions, one expects symbols and the other deeds, and one expects rational negotiation and the other apology, then we have the makings of conflict perpetuation and even escalation, despite the intervention of verbally centered peacemakers who do not understand this problem. If the peacemakers do not train themselves to watch all nonverbal cues, to see the depths and the power of human symbolism, sometimes conscious and sometimes unconscious, then they will miss the most important opportunities for transformation of relationships.

Religious encounters can be rich in the word, the deed, and the symbol. It is our choice, and it is essential that the costs and benefits of these options be understood by religious peacemakers.

The deed addresses the fundamental crux of conflict resolution, the relationship and struggle between justice and peace. Of course, deeds and symbols can go badly as well, and we must be open to the injuries sustained by either side when its gestures are ignored and/or not reciprocated. Clarification of these missed opportunities can and must go on through the use of the word, through dialogue. But correctives can also occur when enemies, made aware of these processes, make up for the failures by reciprocating nonverbal gestures, even when these do not come naturally to their own culture.

In addition to being trained in dialogue and negotiation, religious diplomats and peacemakers must be trained in the detection of other gestures of reconciliation, actions and deeds that mean much more, and are trusted much more, than words. They must train themselves to detect deleterious processes of engagement that result from missed symbolic and nonverbal opportunities, and to invent strategies to consciously align or engage the culturally and religiously familiar conciliatory paths of adversary groups.

As I have stated, however, dialogue is only one subset of the potential of human reconciliation. It tends to favor those who are verbal and aggressive in group encounters. It favors the better educated, and, in my training experience, I have found that a fixation on the exchange of the word tends to frustrate and disempower those who engage in reconciliation through gestures, symbols, emotions, and shared work. But it can and does help some to strategically work toward a more just and comprehensive peace.

Another complication of verbal exchange is that much of dialogue work—religious or secular—becomes overshadowed and even thwarted when the "official" dialogues take over. The latter, while necessary at some point, are deeply disempowering to the vast majority who have no say in the process. We should expect this counterproductive disempowerment as an element in any progress toward official peace, but we should learn how to help people counteract the deleterious effects. Whatever the value of dialogue, official or otherwise, it is only one part of peacemaking. Furthermore, the ups and downs of the official dialogue process tend to hold everyone captive, imprisoned really.

Imagine yourself, for example, in a religious dialogue group. Around you are conditions of absolute misery. On top of this, there are others negotiating for you in "more important" venues of dialogue, whether you asked them to or not, bargaining with their interests in mind, without your input. How much value can you bring yourself to place on your own efforts to dialogue? How much of a price are you paying in your community for your dialogue work?

But what if, while official dialogue proceeds, what you are doing for reconciliation involves deeds, shared deeds between enemies? What if you are doing something concrete to improve the situation? What if you are using the word as prayer or as study or as an expression of care? And let us say your adversaries are partners with you in this. Do you also pay a price with your rejectionists for this cooperation? Yes. Do you feel insignificant and a sense of futility in the face of the more powerful who are negotiating for you in official processes? Not really, because you are actually doing something concrete while they may not be. It is you who have the privilege of engaging in gestures and concrete actions that every day improve someone's life. And when you do it with your enemies you are also creating some reconciliation where there was none. You are not only not disempowered by the official dialogues; you are doing better work than they are, making more progress, and the ups and downs of their negotiation affect you far less. You are culturally, ethically, and psychologically in a much deeper place and much more independent of the vagaries of power relations.

Religious dialogue, however, is here to stay as a method of peace-making and it matters a great deal in many cultures. But here are some caveats on how it should be done. In my years of experience with training people from every religion and every region, the basic sociological reality has remained constant in terms of the dynamics of dialogic encounter. The same is true of the many workshops between enemies that I have witnessed. The more people in a room around a table, the more lies that are spoken, the more distorted the presentation of self, the more tribalistic the psychology of adversaries.

With every decrease in the number of participants, the more truth that is revealed, the more we find emotional honesty, trust, risks taken, confessions made, apologies offered. There are more frank depictions of the past, more creative visions of the future, and more people who act as if they represent themselves rather than some artificial or mythic construct of their group. The best of all seem to be one-on-one dialogic encounters and relationships that develop between adversaries in informal settings.

One simply cannot help noticing the progressive way in which larger and larger groups of human beings tend to behave in a manner that they themselves cannot control. And the less individual control, the more aggression seems to surface. The far end of the spectrum here is a state in which aggression and enemy psychology reach a level of mass hypnosis and a hysteria of other directed rage. One can see this occasionally played out in European soccer events, but the meeting of warriors on the battlefield is the most ancient and perennial example. And I have seen this progressive level of aggression play itself out in many an Arab-Jewish encounter, for example. The greater the number of people, the worse the encounter, particularly because the mediators were totally unprepared for the mob psychology occasioned by large groups. Conversely, the smaller the encounter, the fewer skills are required by the mediators, and the more chance of success.[1]

Dialogue has many permutations, and one interesting development, at least in the interfaith encounter in Israel, has been shared study. Several Israeli interfaith organizations have moved in this direction, sharing numerous study sessions on one another's religions. Yehuda Stolov of the Israel Interfaith Association and the Yakar Institute, for instance, have worked rather brilliantly and tirelessly on these meetings with great success. Study appears to be a rather natural activity for Jews and Arabs trying to get to know each other and may, in fact, create much deeper bonds than Western styles of dialogue about "problems."

The text-centered reverence in Judaism and Islam is a likely cause of this successful mode of interaction, as well as the power and wonder of discovering shared values and traditions *before* one engages in difficult exchanges with adversaries about inflicted injuries. In this case, study, which is in fact dialogic, is also a deed, an act of honoring another's tradition.

We may be witnessing the birth of an indigenous method of conflict resolution that has public joint study and appreciation at its core, while the difficult exchanges on the conflict are reserved for intentional meetings in a very private space. This maximizes the possibility of honesty but minimizes the possibility of dishonor and shame for the respective religious traditions. This may be a formula that will work best for conservative traditions in the region.

The deep resentments and competing mythologies of the Abrahamic families are an important underlying cause of the persistence of the Arab-Israeli conflict, as well as the historical Western confrontation with Islam and the Middle East. Such patterns of study sidestep, if only for a time, those ancient resentments and competitions. They create temporary but sacred time of reconciliation and temporary suspension of judgment. The dialogic encounter is essential to this experience. The theme of oasis creation for shared study is critical here, as it has always been as a first stage of peace.

As a result, many people who participate in these exchanges start mulling over in their minds and hearts a new understanding of these ancient jealousies and possibly new ways to envision monotheism, the Abrahamic family, and the possibilities of coexistence.[2]

It is absolutely true that such religious dialogic exchanges, at least in their public face, often veer away from the most controversial subjects. But there is a unique way in which this is unfolding and yielding great benefits for peace and justice. For example, it was surprising to me that in the winter of 2000, when so many other, problem-centered, Palestinian-Israeli dialogues fell apart, Stolov's interreligious seminars inside Israel not only continued but seemed to become a more intense place of meeting, with rather prominent people from both sides in attendance. Why was it not boycotted? Perhaps because from the beginning it was a place of honoring and equality rather than a place of negotiation. Yes, they avoided politics, but they seemed to be building something deeper.

I have also been informed of more controversial study of late on the sacredness of land, or the importance of Jerusalem in all the faiths. This is a vital and unique way in which religious people are beginning the process of valuating the enemy other's attachment to and care for the same sacred space. We must pay close attention here to these developments. Very religious people do not—and perhaps cannot—approach the enemy other in the same way that, say, a military general might, or a seasoned diplomat, or an attorney. Religious people may be, and are in their public lives, also generals and attorneys and diplomats. But in their religious personalities, in their deepest space of religious authenticity, it may very well be that a different mode of interaction is necessary with the enemy other, or the competing Abrahamic monotheist. An interreligious textual study on the sacredness of Jerusalem, a study of all the texts, traditions, metaphors, and symbols of all peoples, in a respectful, nonbelligerent atmosphere, may be doing things that no rational dialogue or rational bargaining session could ever accomplish.

This may very well be setting the stage for future coexistence in Jerusalem in a way that no rational bargaining can do right now.

Furthermore, even if there are rational breakthroughs on these matters, the latter may impact only a limited elite, whereas the religious re-visioning of sacred spaces has the potential to impact the existential orientation of millions of citizens in many countries. That is why, while I sympathize with those pragmatists who worry that such interfaith exchanges are a smoke screen for inactivity, I beg to differ. Something extraordinary is happening here, and we could magnify this significantly if more people of influence on all sides would have the courage to support this engagement for the masses.

The discovery of study as a path of interfaith meeting and conflict resolution is an extraordinary development in conflict resolution practice, although it is still at an early stage of development, to be sure. This never would have come about in the United States or Europe, despite the fact that the progressive cultures of the latter too often consider themselves the sole font of wisdom on peacemaking. It is true that in the Middle East all three Abrahamic faiths are evolving some very dangerous patterns of antimodernist fundamentalism. But new possibilities are emerging at the same time! It turns out, for example, that for legal and ritual reasons, interfaith prayer is a very problematic gesture for Islamic, Jewish, and Christian traditionalists, despite its revered status in Western circles of peacemaking. Shared prayer involves direct violations of old laws designed to maintain certain boundaries.

At the same time, study is a particularly sanctified practice in Judaism but has old roots in Islam and Christianity as well. There are those who prohibit study of Torah with non-Jews, however, for a variety of historical reasons, involving very bad experiences of use of information gained in shared study to attack the Jewish community or to infiltrate, misinterpret, and missionize the unsuspecting—yet another disastrous injury.[3] Thus, this path will not be for all religious Jews, although reassurances from the Christian community that the past will not be repeated could bring more people in. For those who do participate, this course will yield important results in terms of interreligious understanding. Of course, it will not do much to solve the questions of national boundaries or refugees, but that is not its purpose. All contact is good if it leads to informal relationships that expand the circles of those who come to know and understand the enemy, and who come to resist the destructive mythification of the other.

Destructive mythification is born only in spaces of noncontact, adversarial contact, or ignorance. Shared study, therefore, must become a part of ongoing contact and relationship building on a deeper level. It must yield new intimacies, such as the kind that come from mutual invitations to homes and meetings with families. This has occurred, and it should be emphasized how crucial this is to the success of dialogue that truly is transformative.

This kind of shared study and mutual learning, *not for the purposes of debate or conversion*, is a new form of monotheistic relationship that we must recognize and encourage. This innovation itself in the history of monotheism will engender a certain kind of healing and reconciliation for many deeply religious people.

What are we to make of the more traditional forms of interreligious dialogue? We must ask questions and do more critical research. What models have worked better over the years and what models have failed? Many of the same considerations of conflict resolution theory regarding states or other large entities need to be applied to religious institutions. Strategies such as confidence-building measures and unilateral gestures that one adversary offers to another have all been used at one time or another in interfaith work, but little has been done to document the successes and failures of these methods in religious settings.

There are discernible patterns of progression in interfaith conflict resolution that, if properly identified, may provide a framework of analysis and activism not currently available. For example, in the past decade there has been a remarkable development in the Catholic Church's attitude toward Jews and Judaism that has progressed from papal pronouncements to changes in prayers and educational materials.[4] This is of profound importance because it represents not only a theological shift but also a commitment to change the attitudes of almost a billion believers. The confidence-building character of this development, especially for those who have felt deeply injured by the long history of repression of Jews and Judaism, is remarkable.

This is not to say that there are not still some serious disagreements. Most of the disagreements involve acknowledging past wrongs of the church, and conflict resolution theory and practice would be useful in analyzing both this conflict and its dialogic processes of resolution. Thus, for example, there needs to be greater attention to the perspectival differences of the parties. Many members of the Jewish community point out past sins of the Catholic Church, especially during the Holocaust, such as Pope Pius XII's actions or lack thereof. But members of the Jewish community tend to underemphasize the heroic role of other popes, most noticeably the most recent two, who were particularly committed to the Jews during the Holocaust. For some Jews, this expresses a need to be angry at a long history of mistreatment, but for others, it expresses a desire for apology from the highest sources.

There is an intense cultural difference at work here as well, regarding the evaluation of papal behavior. The sinfulness of a pope is as scandalous and painful in Catholicism as the sinfulness of a *rebbe* would be in Hasidism, maybe more so. But there are a variety of views here in both communities, and for many religious people it is vital to acknowledge with humility that all people and all institutions are capable of sin.

The doctrine of inerrancy causes major problems of interfaith dialogue that go beyond evaluations of a pope. Inerrancy cuts to the heart of the contours of faith, doubt, uncertainty, and the search for unassailable truths in a very murky world. It involves not only questions about popes but also the actions of other major religious figures, prophets, and saviors, as well as flaws of laws enshrined in sacredness.

Asymmetry of power is another important problem in conflict-resolving processes, such as dialogue encounters. Simply stated, adversary groups often come out of circumstances in which one group has more military, economic, political, and/or demographic power than the other group. But the asymmetry also may express itself in the nature of the encounter, its language, structure, and cultural ethos. This skews dialogue and contact between enemy groups as a method of conflict resolution. I would argue that dialogue itself, as a method of peacemaking, is culturally charged, maybe even biased, and may not satisfy or correspond to the best cultural methods that a group may possess for peacemaking and the transformation of relationships between enemies. A peacemaking method can produce asymmetry in and of itself if its execution favors the skills of one group over another's or one subcommunity of each group.

Which language is used is an important subset of asymmetry questions depending on who is comfortable with what language in these encounters and what political statements are being made in a symbolic sense by the use of one language.

Finally, rational negotiations and dialogue can do nothing for the dead, the murdered on all sides. And the murdered weigh on survivors as a burden of indescribable pressure. In nonrational terms, this is the tremendous power that ghosts of the dead play in so many global traditions. Survivor guilt, in my experience, is a principal goad that motivates those who perpetuate conflict. The conflict is a way to keep the memory of the dead alive and the guilt of survival assuaged.

Religious dialogue, to truly move people away from hatred and war, must find prominent ways to "bring into the room" those who are voiceless, politically speaking, such as children, those who are nonverbally inclined, and especially the murdered. They must be honored and considered in order for the dialogic moment not to feel like a betrayal. Religious traditions are eminently capable of bringing these others into a room, but the means by which this happens, through symbol or prayer or shared ethical deed, must be negotiated and arrived at as a part of the relationship- and trust-building tasks of the group encounter.

I want to end with a series of shorter points, some of which summarize earlier comments:

1. It is critical that religious dialogue be an act as well as a verbal communication. That act must be honorable. The act of dialogue must consider and anticipate what constitutes civility and dignity for all the cultures in question. It is critical, therefore, that dialogue participants become part of the process of creating a temporary community that embraces guidelines of treatment and civility, honest conversations, permissible and impermissible means of dealing with hard truths.

2. Dialogue is inherently exclusionary. It excludes everyone who is not in the room. Therefore, it is critical that this be acknowledged and *all the excluded groups* become part of the imagined conversation in terms of ultimate solutions. Otherwise it is an exercise in futility.

3. Shared study and shared practices should be considered as alternative forms of dialogic encounter, or as critical adjuncts to interreligious dialogue.

4. Dialogue can be crucial at the right time and insulting at the wrong time. It can be at the mercy of levels of rage at certain times. It must be time sensitive.

5. Dialogic encounter should always be geared toward a goal that is measurable by the layman participant, especially if he or she is a member of the group that is initiating the fighting. Otherwise it is perceived as, and perhaps is, a substitute for progress.

6. Dialogue should really be a subset of a wide range of informal processes that move the parties toward a transformation of relationship at a deep level. Relationships of respect, sympathy, and dignity engender trust, stimulate novel solutions, and enhance the possibility of moving from good thoughts and words to deeds. Only good deeds create peace and justice ultimately, and only good relationships move us toward good deeds. Interfaith dialogue is good to the degree to which it helps generate good relationships that lead to good deeds, and this is turn will lead to peace and justice.

NOTES

1. Let me emphasize that "success" for me does not mean a happy encounter in which there is no fighting. I think fighting is necessary and important for conflict resolution processes. But these processes need careful guidance and skilled mediation. My disappointment with the large group encounter is that it seems to make impotent many decent intermediaries. There is certainly a range of skills in the field, and some manage large groups better than others. But it is an inescapable fact of dialogic encounter between enemies, and even the educational encounter as such, that large numbers decrease the quality of the encounter. Worse still, I have seen too many people leave a large dialogue convinced—where they were not before—that peace is impossible.

2. For a more in-depth discussion, see Marc Gopin, *Between Eden and Armageddon: The Future of World Religions, Violence, and Peacemaking* (New York and London: Oxford University Press, 2000); Gopin, *Holy War, Holy Peace* (New York and London: Oxford University Press, 2002); and Gopin, "Foreword," in *The Future of Islam and the West*, ed. Shireen Hunter (Westport, Conn.: Praeger, 1998), vi–xi.

3. See Robert Chazan, *Jewish Suffering: The Interplay of Medieval Christian and Jewish Perspectives,* Occasional Papers no. 2, Trinity College (Kalamazoo, Mich.: Medieval Institute Publications, Western Michigan University, 1998). On the general attitude of the church right up to the nineteenth century, in which forced sermons continued, though less frequently, see David Kertzer, *The Kidnapping of Edgardo Mortara* (Newbury Park, Calif.: Vintage Press, 1998).

4. For a full account, see Eugene Fisher, *Faith without Prejudice* (New York: Crossroads Publishing, 1993), chap. 7; Fisher, "Evolution of a Tradition," in *Fifteen Years of Catholic-Jewish Dialogue, 1970–1985,* ed. International Catholic-Jewish Liaison Committee (Rome: Vatican Library, distributed by Lateran University, 1988), chap. 10; and Eugene Fisher and Leon Klenicki, *In Our Time: The Flowering of Jewish-Catholic Dialogue* (Mahwah, N.J.: Paulist Press, 1990). For a Jewish response to the new catechism, see Rabbi Leon Klenicki, "The New Catholic Catechism and the Jews," in *Professional Approaches for Christian Educators* (PACE) 23 (April 1994).

3
Building Bridges
for Interfaith Dialogue

Jaco Cilliers

MY UNDERSTANDING OF INTERFAITH DIALOGUE is based on my involvement in projects and initiatives related to humanitarian relief, development, and peacebuilding undertaken by groups with different religious backgrounds. In my work in several countries I have come across situations in which people from different religious, ethnic, and cultural backgrounds have had to work together to rebuild relationships destroyed by long periods of hatred and conflict. My perspective, therefore, is not necessarily that of religious officials or theologians, who are often—and incorrectly—seen as the only people who should be involved in interfaith dialogue efforts. Rather, my perspective is similar to that of people from different religious backgrounds who are attempting to work together practically to build peace within their communities. Therefore, I do not focus specifically on how groups or individuals who want to talk with one another about religious topics or questions can engage in "the dialogue or discourse on religion" (see Martin 1998).

Interfaith dialogue is not something that can easily be approached within any setting. It is commonly understood that if you want calm, even-tempered conversations between groups, especially if they are from different ethnic and cultural backgrounds, you should avoid bringing up the topic of religion. If one looks at the conflicts in

Northern Ireland, the Middle East, Sri Lanka, India, and Bosnia-Herzegovina, which involve people from different religious traditions, it becomes clear why religion is viewed as one of the primary reasons that conflicts result in violence and war. As Hans Küng points out, it is the case that the "most fanatical and cruelest political struggles are those that have been colored, inspired, and legitimized by religion" (Küng 1986, 442). One of the earliest conflict theorists, Lewis Coser (1956), suggests that conflicts involving religious ideologies are more likely than others to be especially hostile and violent. When religious groups in a conflict eliminate the personal element and perceive themselves as representatives of collectives, their actions tend to become more "radical" and "merciless." These ideological alignments are more often found in "rigid" societies than in "flexible" or "adjustable" ones that provide opportunities for people to engage in dialogue and cooperation.

Successful interfaith dialogue and cooperation in zones of peace can provide a symbolic foundation for peacebuilding efforts, which illustrates that positive cooperation between different religious groups can be achieved. It can also significantly contribute to transforming violent conflicts into opportunities for long-term peace. There is, therefore, a great need for individuals and groups to work together through interfaith dialogue and cooperation to build bridges that transform conflicts and bring peace to societies and communities divided by violence and war.

Although we have to admit that religion is one element of identity that can often contribute significantly to violence, faith should not be seen as an ingredient that fuels the explosion of conflict into violence and war but rather as a foundation that can support efforts to build peace. It is primarily through a process in which groups and individuals first seek a deep understanding of their own religious traditions and then share their religious convictions and traditions with others that meaningful dialogue can be fostered.

GROUNDING INTERFAITH DIALOGUE COMES FROM WITHIN

I strongly feel that it is only when there is a deep understanding of one's own religious beliefs and commitments that progress can be made in achieving true understanding and respect for the religious values and beliefs of others. Engaging in interfaith dialogue does not in any way mean undermining one's own faith or religious tradition. Indeed, interfaith dialogue is constructive only when people become firmly grounded in their own religious traditions and through that process gain a willingness to listen and respect the beliefs of other religions. Since violence characterized by religious differences is so difficult to address, it is very important that people involved in interfaith dialogue firmly plant their roots within their own religious tradition. Interreligious dialogue "cannot be merely a polite meeting of participants from different traditions who engage in swapping superficial information. Rather it must be a sharing from the heart—from the depths of each tradition, solidly rooted in spiritual experiences and supported by centuries of accumulated wisdom" (Cousins 1989, 4).

Grounding the internal discussion on "what within our tradition calls on us to engage in interfaith dialogue" is therefore crucial. This means that the vast majority of work that lays the foundation for interfaith cooperation must take place before the parties meet face-to-face. It is during this process that communities of the same faith traditions formulate and articulate what within their own religious tradition calls them to work with other religious groups and engage in interfaith dialogue. Although this process is often overlooked, it builds the crucial links that will eventually sustain long-term relationships. Interfaith dialogue initiatives are regularly tested and derailed by people from the participating religious traditions who are opposed to any form of interfaith cooperation to bring peace to conflict-ridden societies. By firmly grounding their motivations for conducting interfaith dialogue, the proponents of such dialogue can minimize efforts to disrupt it.

One of the biggest challenges for people involved in interfaith dialogue is to break down the stereotypes of the "other" that exist within their own religious traditions and groups. Religious groups need to first acknowledge and confess their own role in fostering and contributing to injustice and conflict. They must also be willing to confess and ask for forgiveness before they engage in direct interfaith dialogue processes. Opportunities for exchanges between religions are limited, however, and such exchanges need to be structured so that they do not reinforce animosities. Ideally, interfaith dialogue should be supported through peacebuilding efforts that focus on how parties can transform the conflicts that have divided them and contributed to violence.

FOUNDATIONS AND BUILDING BLOCKS
OF INTERFAITH DIALOGUE

Constructive interreligious dialogue is a peacebuilding and conflict transformation process that provides opportunities for people from different religious backgrounds to address central values such as justice, reconciliation, truth, mercy, and forgiveness from their respective traditions. This process can be illustrated metaphorically through the concept of "building bridges for the understanding of interfaith differences." The base of the bridge should be built on the foundations of justice and reconciliation, while the pillars that support the "paths of interfaith dialogue" should be constructed on deep understandings of truth, forgiveness, and mercy as well as peacebuilding and conflict transformation processes and initiatives. Hiskiaz Assefa writes that the religious community should lay the foundation for peace through direct engagement "in building bridges between people separated by conflict, in reconciling adversaries, and in creating community between former enemies" (Assefa 1995, 20).

These concepts should also be viewed within the context and uniqueness of each religious tradition. Every religion has its own perspectives and symbols, and it is important to understand that these values are not universal but have different interpretations within each religious tradition. These concepts and values have complicated meanings and are only briefly explained here to indicate their role and importance in promoting productive interfaith dialogue.

Justice

Efforts to build bridges that can foster peace between different religious groups have to seriously address situations of injustice. As discussed previously, it is important that injustices within societies first be discussed and understood internally to ensure that people who engage in interfaith dialogue can articulate the role that justice plays within their own faith tradition. It is only when there is a clear understanding within a religious tradition of the injustices that contribute to ongoing conflict that attempts can be made to bring groups together to engage in constructive interreligious dialogue.

Justice is defined differently by the world's religious traditions. Justice within the Buddhist tradition is used to point out the need to resist a greater evil and achieve a higher good (see Kraft 1992) or is used to illustrate how the Buddhist principles of the Four Noble Truths resulted from the enlightenment that occurred after the mighty battle that Buddha fought with the forces of injustice and evil (Gage 1995). The Christian tradition has a complex understanding of justice. On the one hand, concepts of justice are used to express fear of the Lord, vengeance, and punishment. On the other hand, another concept of justice calls for a deep commitment to reparation, right relationships, and addressing social inequalities (see United States Catholic Conference, Powers et al. 1994). The concept of "righteousness" is articulated within the Qur'an to refer to the way injustices should be addressed within each person, and also within the world (see Jafta 2000). The interconnectedness of justice and peace and the contribution that justice can make to peace are also emphasized for both the ruler and the believer within Islam (see Kelsay 1993). These examples indicate that it is not often easy to find a common language that captures the complexities of what is meant by the term "justice." They do, however, start to show that there is often a complex understanding of what needs to take place to address injustices and the underlying causes of conflict between people and the world in which they live.

Addressing justice through a faith-based approach was very important for the churches during the apartheid period in South Africa. Although the majority of the population was from the same religious background, the Christian churches were divided into a white and a black church. Apartheid divided people, and the church as such, based on skin color, which resulted in enormous discrepancies and discrimination on economic and social levels. The discussion that took place among certain Christian groups within the country eventually informed the development of the "Kairos Document" (see Kairos Theologians [Group], World Council of Churches, Programme Unit on Justice and Service et al. 1985). This document, published in South Africa in the mid-1980s, pointed out the divisions within the church and illustrated how dehumanizing and unjust the apartheid regime was to the majority of people in the country. The Kairos Document stated that the church cannot talk about reconciliation and forgiveness without addressing injustices within the country. The document also highlighted that dialogue between the black and white churches in South Africa must seriously address the structural injustices brought about by apartheid. During the midst of the conflict in South Africa, religious groups and leaders therefore did not engage in religious dialogue across the white-black divide without first addressing justice and the situation of the marginalized majority within the country. The "internal discussions" that took place around the concept of justice within the Christian churches in South Africa eventually led to a deeper internal search that provided the basis for the important role the church played in the country's peace process.

Reconciliation

The other foundation that sustains the bridge for interfaith dialogue is reconciliation. The Kairos Document explained that the purpose of reconciliation within the South African context had to be very closely linked to the promotion of justice. As indicated by John de Gruchy (1997, 22), "the Kairos theologians were right to criticize cheap reconciliation, for reconciliation cannot be achieved without justice being done to the oppressed."

The process of reconciliation implies that people who want to engage in interfaith cooperation should be prepared to reflect critically on their own religious tradition. They should also contemplate what place their own religious tradition assigns to people of other faith traditions. The process of reconciliation also emphasizes the need to restore relationships and to engage in processes that can lead to social and spiritual healing.

Reconciliation has to be sustained over long periods. This requires creating opportunities in which groups can first discover their own motivations for reconciling with people and groups of other religions. Unfortunately, in many recent postaccord conflicts, such as in Bosnia-Herzegovina, Kosovo, and East Timor, religious and ethnic communities divided by violence and war are required by the international community to work immediately on "reconciliation projects" that include people from all sides of the conflict. This is often unreasonable and unrealistic. There is a need for people affected by war and violence to have time not only to heal but also to work on their own willingness to engage face-to-face with those with whom they were fighting.

While working and living in Bosnia-Herzegovina, I had the opportunity to be part of an initiative that worked with teachers within a town that was split by the war. The town was divided by ethnic and religious identity, with the Muslim and Catholic communities deeply entrenched in their mutual animosity. Although those involved in the initiative were eager to bring the two groups together, they quickly realized that this would be unrealistic. A decision therefore was made to work separately with a group of teachers in each community through various conflict transformation trainings and to help them with other small initiatives. Another decision was made not to require them to meet together before they were ready to make that commitment themselves. Nearly four years later, during one of my return trips to Bosnia-Herzegovina, I was enthusiastically approached by one of the teachers, who told me that the two groups of teachers had been able to meet for the first time only two weeks before. She reminded me of the process we had started and indicated that it was often very frustrating for her that the two sides never met jointly over the four-year period. However, she had come to realize that during this time they had gone through a process that had strengthened their own faith identity, which she felt had better prepared her for the first reconciliation meeting that took place. Bernard Haring (1986, 4) indicates that it is impossible to "help the sick if we do not recognize what is sick in ourselves and have not learned to accept the others as sick people." The foundation of any reconciliation process must be grounded within a deep understanding of what has to change within ourselves before attempts are made to focus on reconciliation with the "other."

Interfaith dialogue efforts cannot be effective if reconciliation initiatives do not take place within religious groups as well as between individuals and religious groups who have been in conflict with one another. Reconciliation implies that rebuilding or reestablishing communication and relationships between former enemies must take place.

It also means that stereotypes of the other need to change and that productive images and descriptions of other religious groups need to emerge through the fostering of mutual respect and trust. The importance of reconciliation within interfaith dialogue efforts is therefore of the utmost importance within societies divided by violence and protracted conflicts.

ADDITIONAL PILLARS OF INTERFAITH DIALOGUE

Forgiveness

The issue that is often the most difficult to address during interfaith dialogue is how groups and individuals who have been the victims of injustice can show mercy or forgiveness to their persecutors. Joseph Montville (1993, 112) points out that "healing and reconciliation in violent ethnic and religious conflicts depend on a process of transactional contrition and forgiveness between aggressors and victims which is indispensable to the establishment of a new relationship based on mutual acceptance and reasonable trust. The process depends on a joint analysis of the history of the conflict, recognition of injustices and resulting historic wounds, and acceptance of moral responsibility where due." The role that religious traditions can play in this process is very important. For instance, there is a complex but very deep conviction within the religious traditions of the Abrahamic faiths that God is forgiving and compassionate and that believers are required to show forgiveness to those with whom they are in conflict. Though there are certainly differences among the interpretations, there is a common understanding within these traditions that forgiveness is central to the way people should deal with one another, is how relationships should be rebuilt, and is how the virtue and mercy of God are expressed through humans (see Gopin 2001; Saiyidian 1976; Helmick and Peterson 2001).

The process of forgiveness is not a process in which parties are required to simply forgive and forget. Neither should mercy be seen as simply an act of kindness that the victim should undertake. These acts or processes cannot take place in isolation; they must occur at the same time that the perpetrator seriously considers the injustices visited on the victim and constructively addresses situations of wrongdoing. How to deal with restitution and healing should also be central to the larger discussion of what can be done to enhance elements of forgiveness.

Truth

A common misperception in interfaith dialogue is that cooperation can easily break down when people discover that what is "true" in their own religion opposes what is "true" in the other religious tradition. Those engaged in interfaith dialogue should come to the table with the understanding that differences do exist and that the objective is not to "correct" but to hear and listen to the other side.

The purpose of focusing on truth during interfaith dialogue is to seek and discover the "truths" within a religious tradition that form identity and provide opportunities for cooperation and engaging in joint discovery of different traditions. The fact that religions, which usually have at their core a promotion of tolerance and peace, have been exploited to carry out violence clearly indicates that individuals and groups have not discovered the true "peace message" that is inherent in almost every religion. This is illustrated by Anantanand Rambachan (1998), who refers to the journey that Swami Vivekananda took at the end of the nineteenth century to discover the true meaning of the Hindu religion and how that journey eventually led to a commitment to interfaith dialogue. Rambachan points out that Vivekananda "is arguing that all religions are true, and that religious growth is not from error to truth, but from lower to higher truth . . . inter-religious dialogue does not seem possible without the participants possessing commitment to a particular understanding of the universe and feeling that this understanding is relevant for all people. Dialogue must be founded on religious conviction" (Rambachan 1998, 17–18).

It is more important for people engaged in interfaith dialogue to have a joint discovery of what is "true and right" than to achieve a "religious victory" as if the dialogue were a debate (see Martin 1998). Part of the "truth discovery process" is for groups from different religious traditions to understand how they can share their values in such a way that the true message of their faith benefits people from other faith traditions. The search for truth within a religious tradition should therefore focus not only on what is found within the religious tradition, but also on how believers can engage in constructively sharing experiences through interreligious dialogue.

Conflict Transformation and Peacebuilding

Interreligious dialogue often creates unique possibilities to enhance cooperation between groups and communities divided by conflict. Providing opportunities for this to take place is often very difficult to accomplish. However, processes found within the practice and experience of conflict transformation and peacebuilding can significantly support these types of opportunities. Peacebuilding and conflict transformation processes provide examples of what can be done to rebuild the emotional and structural relationships between parties, which are so crucial during interfaith dialogue. The transformation that is needed to enhance true interfaith dialogue must occur at an interpersonal level as well as at a structural level. There is also a need to transform "the socio-economic and political structures to bring about an authentic order of peace and justice" (Haring 1986, 9).

Numerous factors have to be taken into consideration when initiatives are undertaken to bring people divided by violence and different religious traditions together to engage in interfaith dialogue and cooperation. There is a need to understand the "bigger picture" while also focusing on concrete issues and strengthening relationships that can build trust. As one of the leading theorists and practitioners on conflict transformation and peacebuilding, John Paul Lederach (1995, 1997) indicates that peacebuilding implies both a "descriptive" and a "prescriptive" understanding of change. Descriptively, peacebuilding refers to the various dynamics that characterize conflicts. These conflict dynamics may include the patterns, relationships, communication, issues, and perceptions that impact or arise from conflicts exacerbated by interfaith differences. Prescriptively, peacebuilding emphasizes a comprehensive or holistic approach to dealing with conflict. Consideration must also be given to addressing the underlying causes of violence and the goals and motivations of those interested in getting involved in the conflict.

Lederach (1995) points out that efforts to engage in cooperation and dialogue and to transform conflicts brought about by deep ethnic and religious divisions must include three elements. First, there must be a comprehensive plan to deal with both "short- and long-term transformation." This implies creating measures to address immediate concerns but also keeps in mind the importance of building long-term relationships by addressing the underlying causes of the conflict. The parties to the conflict must be made aware of their mutual dependence and must explore various methods to improve trust between them. Interfaith dialogue initiatives should therefore focus not only on what can be done to structure the dialogue process as constructively as possible, but also on what can be done to sustain cooperation and relationships across longer periods such as decades.

Second, Lederach stresses that conflict transformation and peacebuilding must work toward establishing an "infrastructure for peace." This implies the creation of various peace processes and mechanisms, designed according to the actors and leadership levels within a given society. As was mentioned earlier, it is often assumed that only religious officials should undertake interfaith dialogue. To be sure, they are an important element in such dialogue, but by themselves they cannot sustain peacebuilding efforts. Actors and people from various religious backgrounds should also be involved in joint peacebuilding efforts that can strengthen relationships at various leadership levels.

Third, Lederach argues that attention must be given to building a "peace constituency" based on indigenous and appropriate cultural methods and techniques. Efforts to initiate interfaith cooperation and dialogue must explore suitable local processes and initiatives that are responsive to the local context. It is only when these initiatives and structures are supported and sustained by the actors and parties involved in interfaith dialogue that interfaith efforts can constructively contribute to peace.

CONCLUSION

Many of the traditional approaches to interfaith dialogue have assumed that it can be successful only if agreements are reached about amorphous concepts and themes that various traditions may have in common. These approaches have also assumed that participants have to "weaken" or "compromise" elements of their own faith. Throughout this chapter, I have argued that this is not necessarily constructive for engaging in interfaith understanding and dialogue. It is only when participants have a deep understanding of their own religious traditions and are willing to learn and recognize the richness of other religious traditions that constructive cooperation can take place between groups from different faiths. Adam Curle (1990) points out that "who we are" refers to "private peacemaking" while "what we do" must be seen as "public peacemaking." These two roles are also central to interfaith dialogue efforts. It is only when there is a true understanding of "who we are" and what we bring to the process of interfaith dialogue that progress can be made toward constructively addressing "what we do" through face-to-face interfaith peacemaking efforts.

This chapter has also outlined how a deep commitment to justice, reconciliation, truth, and forgiveness can build bridges that support interfaith dialogue. Religious groups are often taken advantage of by political, economic, or social forces that are out to promote their own fanaticism and intolerance. Religious groups can resist such forces only when they are deeply grounded in their religious traditions around the elements of justice, reconciliation, truth, and forgiveness; only then can individuals and groups involved in interfaith dialogue and cooperation efforts work toward building long-term peace. By also including in this dialogue process elements found within the practice and theory of conflict transformation and peacebuilding, individuals and groups can significantly increase their chances of creating a constructive interfaith dialogue. A major challenge of interfaith cooperation is to involve people from all walks of life in the dialogue process. It is important to build relationships across various levels to strengthen opportunities for interfaith dialogue and collaboration in zones of peace.

REFERENCES

Assefa, Hizkias. 1995. *Peace and Reconciliation as a Paradigm.* Nairobi: Nairobi Peace Initiative.

Coser, Lewis A. 1956. *The Functions of Social Conflict.* Glencoe, N.Y.: Free Press.

Cousins, E. H. 1989. "Interreligious Dialogue: The Spiritual Journey of Our Time." In *Interreligious Dialogue: Voices from a New Frontier,* ed. M. Darrol Bryant and Frank Flinn. New York: Paragon House.

Curle, Adam. 1990. *Tools for Transformation: A Personal Study.* Stroud, U.K.: Hawthorn Press.

De Gruchy, John W. 1997. "The Dialectic of Reconciliation: Church and the Transition to Democracy in South Africa." In *The Reconciliation of Peoples: Challenges to the Church,* ed. G. Baum and H. Wells. New York: Orbis Books.

Gage, Richard L. 1995. *Choose Peace: A Dialogue between Johan Galtung and Daisaku Ikeda.* London: Pluto Press.

Gopin, Marc. 2001. "Forgiveness as an Element of Conflict Resolution in Religious Cultures: Walking the Tightrope of Reconciliation and Justice." In *Reconciliation, Justice, and Coexistence: Theory and Practice,* ed. Mohammed Abu-Nimer. Lanham, Md.: Lexington Books, 87–99.

Haring, Bernard. 1986. *The Healing Power of Peace and Nonviolence.* New York: Paulist Press.

Helmick, Raymond G., and Rodney L. Peterson. 2001. *Forgiveness and Reconciliation: Religion, Public Policy, and Conflict Transformation.* Philadelphia: Templeton Foundation Press.

Jafta, L. 2000. "Eco-Human Justice and Well-Being." In *Race and Reconciliation in South Africa,* ed. William E. Van Vugt and G. Daan Cloete. Lanham, Md.: Lexington Books.

Kairos Theologians (Group), World Council of Churches, Programme Unit on Justice and Service et al. 1985. *Challenge to the Church: A Theological Comment on the Political Crisis in South Africa: The Kairos Document and Commentaries.* Geneva: World Council of Churches.

Kelsay, John. 1993. *Islam and War: A Study in Comparative Ethics.* Louisville: Westminster/John Knox Press.

Kraft, Kenneth L. 1992. *Inner Peace, World Peace: Essays on Buddhism and Nonviolence.* Albany: State University of New York Press.

Küng, Hans. 1986. *Christianity and the World Religions: Paths of Dialogue with Islam, Hinduism, and Buddhism.* Garden City, N.Y.: Doubleday.

Lederach, John Paul. 1995. "Conflict Transformation in Protracted Internal Conflicts: The Case for a Comprehensive Framework." In *Conflict Transformation,* ed. Kumar Rupesinghe. New York: St. Martin's Press, xiv, 270.

———. 1997. *Building Peace: Sustainable Reconciliation in Divided Societies.* Washington, D.C.: United States Institute of Peace Press.

Martin, Terence J. 1998. *Living Words: Studies in Dialogues about Religion.* Atlanta, Ga.: Scholars Press.

Montville, Joseph V. 1993. "The Healing Function of Political Conflict Resolution." In *Conflict Resolution Theory and Practice: Integration and Application,* ed. Dennis J. D. Sandole and Hugo Van der Merwe. Manchester, U.K.: Manchester University Press, 112–127.

Rambachan, Anantanand. 1998. "Swami Vivekananda: A Hindu Model for Interreligious Dialogue." In *Interreligious Dialogue: Voices from a New Frontier,* ed. M. D. Bryant and F. Flinn. New York: Paragon House.

Saiyidian, K. G. 1976. *Islam, the Religion of Peace: Islam and Modern Age Society.* New Delhi: Leaders Press.

United States Catholic Conference, G. F. Powers et al. 1994. *Peacemaking: Moral and Policy Challenges for a New World.* Washington, D.C.: United States Catholic Conference.

Part II
The Practice of Dialogue: Case Studies

4

American Jews, Christians, and Muslims Working Together for Peace in the Middle East

Ronald Young

S HALOM, SALAAM, PEACE! In all three traditions—Jewish, Islamic, and Christian—the pursuit of peace is fundamental to doing God's will. Yet when it comes to working for peace between the Arab states, Israel, and the Palestinians, interfaith cooperation has been practically nonexistent. Since 1987, however, several hundred American Jewish, Christian, and Muslim leaders have been working together in the U.S. Interreligious Committee for Peace in the Middle East.

Why is cooperation usually so difficult? What makes interfaith work for Middle East peace more possible today? What are the challenges to cooperation in each of the three communities? Why is interfaith cooperation for peace important?

HISTORICAL OBSTACLES AND NEW HOPES

In the decades since the founding of modern-day Israel and the first Arab-Israeli war in 1948, work for peace in the Middle East has confronted multiple obstacles. First, based on the bitter history of the conflict and what for years were mutually exclusive goals of the two sides—that is, security for Israel versus liberation of all of Palestine—most people have been profoundly pessimistic about the prospects for a negotiated peace. Indeed, it is not an exaggeration to say that for several decades each side wanted the other to disappear. Arabs in general and Palestinians in particular refused to recognize the state of Israel, and Israeli Jews refused to acknowledge Palestinians as a people with the right of national self-determination in the same small land claimed by Jews as their homeland. The bitterness and pessimism engendered tended to generate passionate partisanship or cynical detachment rather than committed activism to help resolve the conflict.

A second obstacle is the complexity of the conflict. Partisan loyalty to a particular side and the tendency to simplify, if not mythologize, the issues led many people to characterize the conflict in terms of "right" versus "wrong." Unfortunately, many persons inclined to work for justice and peace often seem to prefer to view conflicts in black-and-white terms. In fact, understanding the Arab-Israeli-Palestinian conflict requires developing an appreciation for the fact that both sides present compelling moral and historical claims and both peoples—Jews and Palestinians—have endured terrible suffering.

A third obstacle, especially challenging to interfaith work for peace, is the way in which addressing issues in the Middle East causes all of us—Jews, Christians, and Muslims—to confront some of our deepest fears and most persistent prejudices about one another. Moreover, it must be acknowledged that, tragically, religion has served as often to fuel the Arab-Israeli-Palestinian conflict as it has to help resolve it.

Developments in the past twenty-plus years—including the Camp David treaty between Egypt and Israel (1979), the war in Lebanon (1982), the Palestinian uprising (1987), the end of the Cold War and the beginning of U.S.-Soviet cooperation at the Madrid Conference (1991), the Oslo-mediated, Israeli-PLO Declaration of Principles (1993), and the peace treaty between Israel and Jordan (1994)—have had the effect of focusing attention more clearly on the issues that must be resolved and of tempering pessimism about the prospects for a comprehensive peace. In the context of a conflict in which each side wanted the other to disappear, the agreement and handshake between Prime Minister Yitzhak Rabin and Chairman Yasir Arafat represented an extraordinary, even miraculous, irreversible breakthrough.

In theory, the theological and moral case for interfaith cooperation for peace may always have been strong, but it was not until there was evidence that peace was possible that American Jewish, Christian, and Muslim leaders began to explore working together. For years, interfaith dialogue (which for the most part meant Jewish-Christian dialogue) in the United States consistently avoided addressing the Middle East. It is still the case today that interfaith work more often seeks to avoid or suppress conflict over issues in the Middle East than to engage in honest and self-critical dialogue.

While religious leaders who founded the U.S. Interreligious Committee in 1987 believed that "working for peace is not optional, but fundamental to our faith," the practical inspiration for this initiative came from Israelis, Palestinians, and other Arabs who had begun to dialogue and to develop a vision of peace. Interfaith leadership trips to Israel, the West Bank and Gaza, Egypt, Jordan, and Syria in 1985 and 1986 played an essential role in laying a foundation for formation of the committee. Prominent Israelis and prominent Arabs were keynote speakers at the unpublicized founding meeting of the committee in June 1987 and at the first public meeting in January 1988. The founding of the committee and its work since then reflect positive change in the Middle East, which signals growing prospects for development of a peace process and the recognition that interreligious cooperation here could help the United States play an active and creative role in that process.

Yet, to be honest, interreligious cooperation for peace in the Middle East is very difficult work. Based on the experience of working with the committee since 1987, what are some of the issues or obstacles to cooperation for persons in each of the three communities? While discussing the challenges can be discouraging to efforts for cooperation, unless the efforts are realistic and sensitive they will most likely generate frustration and fail.

CHALLENGES TO COOPERATION FOR PEACE

Issues for American Jews

During the Palestinian uprising of 1987, an American rabbi and his seven-year-old son were watching television evening news showing Israeli soldiers in Gaza chasing and beating Palestinian youth who had thrown stones at their patrol. The rabbi's son asked his father, "Why are the soldiers beating those Jewish kids?" When the boy's father expressed surprise and told his son that the youth were Palestinians and that the soldiers were Jewish, the boy exclaimed, "That couldn't be."

For Jews, who have experienced centuries of prejudice and persecution, culminating only sixty years ago in the Holocaust, the idea of Jews as victims is embedded very deeply in the psyche, almost as a matter of self-definition. This makes it extremely difficult for many Jews to accept that, like all peoples who have gained power, Israeli Jews have become victimizers as well as victims.

Opinion polls have consistently shown since the early 1990s that most American Jews support the Palestinian people's right of self-determination and the idea of Israel giving up most of the West Bank and Gaza to a Palestinian state, in exchange for secure borders and peaceful relations. At the same time, many Jews still are reluctant to criticize Israel in public, outside the Jewish community. This tendency reflects deep, persistent fears among Jews, arising from their unique history, that such criticism might erode non-Jewish support for Israel (or contribute to latent anti-Jewish attitudes), which could eventually endanger Israel's survival.

Efforts by American Jews to dialogue and cooperate with Palestinian Americans inevitably means listening to the personal and family histories of Palestinians, and this means being willing to confront the other side of the incredible and often idealized story of Israel's creation out of the ashes of the Holocaust. The myth of "a land without a people for a people without a land" does not hold up for long when the story of the Palestinian people is acknowledged. The Palestinians' word for the creation of Israel is *nakhba*, which means the "disaster," referring to the defeat and dispersal of the Palestinian people from what had been their homeland for centuries. In the long run, confronting the Palestinian story and addressing the moral complexities of modern Israel's creation may be liberating for Jews, but in the meantime, obviously, it is very difficult and painful.

For Jews, working with non-Jews for peace in the Middle East means acknowledging that Israel's fate depends in no small measure on the goodwill and support of the United States and world community, which only sixty years ago acquiesced in the abandonment of the Jews. Not surprisingly, Jews relate to this reality of dependence on others with substantial wariness, especially when it comes to issues affecting the survival of Israel.

Issues for Arab American Christians and Muslim Americans

Despite recent progress, Arab Americans, both Christian and Muslim, and Muslim Americans are still in the process of emerging publicly as organized communities in the United States. It should not be surprising that, as their communities are in the process of gaining public recognition and acceptance, many Arab Americans and Muslim Americans are wary of becoming involved in an issue as controversial and sensitive as the Arab-Israeli-Palestinian conflict, especially when they perceive a strong public and political bias in favor of Israel.

Arab Americans and Muslim Americans are painfully aware of how much ignorance and prejudice exist in our society toward the Arab world and toward Islam. Most have direct personal experiences of negative stereotyping and prejudice, and some have experienced verbal and even violent, physical abuse. During the Persian Gulf War Arab Americans and Muslim Americans were targeted by the FBI for selective investigations, and there were numerous incidents of abuse by other citizens. After the bombing of the federal office building in Oklahoma City, many people, including those in the media, immediately speculated that it was the work of terrorists from the Middle East. Mosques in several U.S. cities have been vandalized and burned. Even when churches and synagogues have reached out, as many have, to defend the rights of Arab and Muslim Americans, there is very little inclination to cooperate in addressing the Arab-Israeli-Palestinian conflict.

For Arab Christians and Muslims of Middle Eastern origin, discussion of the Middle East brings up a lot of painful history—history that non-Arabs and non-Muslims tend to forget—including the

Crusades and the Inquisition, rule by the Ottoman Empire, long periods of European colonial rule, and, since 1948, the series of humiliating wars with Israel. Remembering the period of the Golden Age less than a millennium ago, when Arab-Muslim societies were the source of some of the greatest achievements of civilization, many Arabs still have trouble understanding what happened to Arab greatness. It is even harder for Arab Americans to confront this history when they know that the vast majority of Americans have very little appreciation for Arab culture and history.

Furthermore, while most Arab Americans—indeed most Arabs—acknowledge among themselves that Arab suffering in recent decades has resulted in part from tragic failures in Arab leadership, they (like Jews) fear that any self-critical views they express outside their community will simply reinforce existing prejudices about and negative stereotypes of Arabs.

For Palestinian Americans, whether Christian or Muslim, working for peace with Jewish Americans inevitably involves listening to the painful history of Jewish suffering and to the fears Jews have of Palestinians and other Arabs, based on the decades of Arab hostility to Israel. For most Palestinian Americans, who have their own history of painful suffering as a result of the creation of Israel, this is simply too much. With family members still living as refugees or still suffering under Israeli occupation in the West Bank and Gaza, it is very difficult for many Palestinian Americans to be actively sympathetic to the sufferings and fears of Jews.

Issues for Non-Arab American Christians

A basic challenge for non-Arab American Christians is to resist the temptation of thinking that we come to this conflict with clean hands. A particularly awful, perhaps apocryphal, example of this attitude is reflected in the view of a U.S. (Christian) ambassador in the 1950s who is reported to have blurted out in a moment of frustration over the Middle East conflict, "If only Arabs and Jews would learn to resolve their conflict like good Christians."

It is essential that Christians acknowledge their history with the Jewish people and with Arabs and Muslims, much of which is a history of intolerance, persecution, and colonial rule, often explicitly or at least implicitly based on interpretations of Christian teachings. It is equally essential that Christians acknowledge and challenge the persistent underlying prejudices that still exist today among Christians toward Jews and toward Arabs and Muslims.

Most Christians tend to think of Jews as another religious group or, as one rabbi put it, as "Unitarians who happen to speak Hebrew." Many implicitly reject or at least do not understand the concept of Jewish peoplehood, which is the fundamental source of moral legitimacy for Jewish nationalism—that is, Zionism. This helps to explain why for the most part American Christians were silent about the UN resolution, only recently repudiated, that equated Zionism with racism.

Many American Christians tend to ignore the rich diversity and strong differences of opinion among Israeli Jews. Some Christians react defensively on behalf of Jews and label any criticism of Israel as anti-Jewish. Other Christians use criticism of Israeli policies to express hostility toward Israel, often thinly disguising much deeper prejudice and resentment toward Jews.

On the other side, examples of ignorance and prejudice toward Arabs and Muslims are even more common. Many American Christians still carry very negative stereotypes of Arabs and Muslims. Specifically, in relation to the Arab-Israeli-Palestinian conflict, for years most American Christians equated the Palestine Liberation Organization (PLO) with terrorism, thus denying the PLO's legitimacy, even though this often implicitly meant denying the basic legitimacy of the Palestinian people's right of self-determination in their own land. Just as Jews felt hurt and angry when Zionism was equated with racism, so Arabs have felt when the PLO or Palestinians have been equated with terrorism.

Many American Christians tend to be ignorant about Arab Christians and even more uninformed about Muslims. Most have little or no knowledge of the teachings in the Qur'an. While there has been progress since the Holocaust in the development of positive Christian theology toward the Jewish people, there are only the barest beginnings of a constructive Christian theology toward Islam.

Another challenge for non-Arab American Christians is that often the particular experience or context that first motivated their interest in the Middle East then blinds them to other dimensions of the conflict. Many Christian scholars and others who focused on Christian responsibility for anti-Semitism and the Holocaust largely ignored the suffering of Palestinians. Christians primarily interested in Christian holy sites or in viewing events in the Middle East as "fulfillment of prophecies" tend to ignore the contemporary peoples—Jews and Arabs—and their hopes for the future. Christians who have become active on the Middle East primarily out of a sense of solidarity with the suffering of Palestinians tend to draw misguided analogies to liberation struggles in Central America or South Africa, often implicitly rejecting the moral legitimacy of the creation of Israel and the long-frustrated rights of Israelis to recognition and security from their neighbors.

WHY INTERFAITH COOPERATION IS IMPORTANT

The challenges to interfaith cooperation for peace in the Middle East are daunting. When peace negotiations are making progress, cooperation becomes more feasible. But when the peace process breaks down and violence erupts, the challenges to cooperation once again seem overwhelming. This was the situation in late 2000 as violent confrontation escalated between Israelis and Palestinians. As when the committee was first formed, so during this period examples of Israelis and Palestinians cooperating played an important role in tempering narrow partisanship by American Jews, Christians, and Muslims.

In April 2001 the Palestinian Lutheran bishop in Jerusalem issued an urgent appeal for American Christians to help end the violent confrontation and Israeli occupation; his appeal explicitly called on Christians to work with Muslims and *with Jews* seeking peace. An Israeli Orthodox Jewish father, whose soldier son had been kidnapped and killed by the radical Palestinian group Hamas, organized bereaved Israeli and Palestinian parents to advocate for completing the peace process. Even after months of violent confrontation several prominent Palestinian and Israeli political leaders and peace activists continued to meet together privately to explore how to restart negotiations for peace.

Why, when violent confrontation causes most people to see things from one side only, do some Israelis and Palestinians continue to work together? What are the implications for us as Americans? First, these Israelis and Palestinians, striving to be politically realistic, recognize that it is impossible to understand what is happening and why without listening to the experiences and perceptions of people on the other side. Second, meeting with each other is even more important in times of violent confrontation to counteract the tendency to see only the worst about the other side. Third, by working together Israelis and Palestinians keep alive the common vision of peace, that is, Israel and a Palestinian state living side by side, a vision that still can generate majority support on both sides. Fourth, Israelis and Palestinians working together—knowing that there are partners for peace on the other side and modeling negotiations for peace—are stronger and more effective politically than if they work completely separately. At a deeper level some persons involved in this common work believe they are commanded by their faith to work together for peace, even when it is extremely difficult to do so. Israelis and Palestinians work together because they believe doing so generates not only greater moral clarity but also greater political realism.

These reasons for working together apply equally to the situation of American Christians, Jews, and Muslims who want to work for peace in the Middle East. And yet, for the most part, our communities still tend to work separately and sometimes in conflict with one another. There is a tendency, especially during a period of violent confrontation, simply to mirror the pain and anger of people on the side of the conflict with which we feel most connected. That response, while understandable, lacks the moral clarity and political realism needed to be helpful. We need actively and insistently to seek each other out and to listen to each other. And we need to struggle to find common, politically realistic advocacy positions. Working together for peace not only reflects fundamental imperatives in our religious traditions but also offers the best practical prospect of enabling us to influence our own government to help revive forward movement toward negotiated, comprehensive, and lasting peace in the Middle East. This is a goal that should evoke a profound sense of humility and determination in all of us.

5

Contributions of Interfaith Dialogue to Peacebuilding in the Former Yugoslavia

David Steele

*P*EACEBUILDING INCLUDES A WIDE RANGE OF ACTIVITIES that contribute toward the transformation of society into a just and harmonious order and the development of an infrastructure capable of maintaining this arrangement. This multifaceted process begins with prewar conflict prevention and ends with postwar reconstruction. In all the stages of conflict, interested actors, both institutions and individuals, can perform a variety of constructive functions. These intervention roles include observer, educator, advocate, and intermediary. The observer's role is to be a vigilant presence that can report, or sometimes even prevent, violence and other forms of injustice. The educator's role is to raise the population's awareness regarding injustice and misperception, nourish positive values, promote healing, and train people in conflict intervention skills. The advocate's role is to actively promote, through nonviolent forms of pressure (e.g., public statements, lobbying, and demonstrations), a particular outcome to the conflict, a specific process for resolving the conflict, or the interests of one party to the conflict. The intermediary's role is to act as a go-between, facilitating communication through message carrying or face-to-face encounter, in order to build better relationships (through conciliation efforts) or resolve specific disputes (using mediation techniques).

The purpose of this chapter is to assess the kinds of religiously motivated intervention, in particular those performed in the context of interfaith dialogue and collaboration, that have made the best contribution to peacebuilding in the former Yugoslavia. One can point to many examples of each of the intervention roles described here. The education role has been most important. As director of a project on religion and conflict resolution at the Center for Strategic and International Studies (CSIS) in Washington, D.C., this author has personally led numerous seminars, often in cooperation with local partners, with the express purpose of promoting healing, nourishing faith-based values, addressing misperceptions, and teaching conflict resolution skills. In addition to the seminars, participants (along with other people of faith) have frequently become involved in other educational activities, many times taking the initiative to develop roundtable discussions, literature, media coverage, support groups, and interfaith summer schools that have helped to lay a foundation for peacebuilding. As a result of the seminars, participants have also been empowered to perform the other intervention roles. Some participants in seminars in Bosnia-Herzegovina, including Bishop Hrisistom, the Serbian Orthodox bishop of Bihać-Petrovac, have performed the observer role by accompanying refugees in order to prevent acts of violence against them as they returned to their homes. Following a seminar on problem solving, held in Fojnica, Bosnia, in May 1996, the head imam from that Muslim city, Menšur Pasalic, successfully advocated for the return of Croatian refugees and has since mediated disputes between the returnees and their neighbors. All the attendees at a seminar in Šipovo, in the Bosnian Serb Republic, in March 2000, participated in outcome and process advocacy by requesting that their discussion of corruption be aired on public television. They challenged both political and religious leadership, as well as ordinary citizens, to take a stand against corruption, calling for the authorities to adopt moral statements, better laws, tighter enforcement, and stronger incentive measures. They called for a multireligious movement to confront this corruption. These examples are simply a few of the many instances in which people of faith in the former Yugoslavia have contributed to peacebuilding.

In order to properly assess the effectiveness of interfaith dialogue and collaboration in the process of peacebuilding, we must examine prerequisites for success, guidelines for an effective dialogue process, essential follow-up measures, and ways to build supportive institutional structures.

PREREQUISITES FOR SUCCESS

The first prerequisite for success is to have a clear purpose. Having clear goals, however, is distinct from having the power to transform society. One of the primary contributions that people from the Abrahamic faith traditions can bring to peacebuilding is their sense of dependence on God. When trust is placed in the transforming power of God to bring justice or reconciliation, this perspective frees the true person of faith from the need for coercive action to achieve some social ideal. Success, therefore, is not measured by the degree to which one can change the situation. The goal of transforming any social process is secondary to the aim of faithfulness to God's purposes. For people of faith, then, pursuit of any aspiration should be rooted in an awareness of participation in the action of God. Such an awareness offers clear purpose and motivation but discourages manipulation in the effort to carry out any peacebuilding activity.

This important caveat now articulated, it is important to return to the need to formulate a clear purpose, albeit one that is in line, to the best of one's understanding, with the purposes of God. In the Abrahamic tradition that forms the basis of all the faith communities found in the former Yugoslavia, there are some universal values that should inform any peacebuilding efforts. For people of faith, the most basic value is placed in developing honest, loving, and holistic relationships with God and neighbor. When war confronts the person of faith with the catastrophic breakdown of neighborly love, the primary call is to reverse the process by redeveloping constructive relationships with one's adversary. This rebuilding of relationships is more important than solving particular social problems, resolving specific disputes, or issuing public statements of agreement or intent. The rebuilding of community is the crucial beginning point in religiously motivated peacebuilding. Finding ways to effectively handle grievances, reconcile differences, and heal the wounds of war through interfaith dialogue, therefore, is an essential process at the very center of peacebuilding.

If interfaith dialogue is to be an effective tool in rebuilding a fractured community, we must start with the question of whom to invite to such a process. When trust is broken so deeply, effective interfaith dialogue requires people who are open to examination of all the dynamics of a conflicted relationship and who are committed to working through the difficulties with others of goodwill. Finding participants who are likely to agree to attend a series of interfaith encounters is very important, since continued encounter is necessary for the building of community. Although such a commitment is usually too much to expect at the very beginning, it has frequently happened that a core of people from an initial interfaith dialogue session has eventually formed the nucleus from which new interfaith peacebuilding institutions have been formed. This has been my experience in Serbia, Croatia, and Bosnia-Herzegovina.

In addition to finding open and committed people, it is important to invite people who can influence others. Although those at the top of the religious hierarchies are prominent individuals, they frequently are not as receptive to sustained interfaith dialogue, nor do they have the time to make a commitment to it. However, middle-level people are often open, available, and able to influence both up and down the social ladder. These middle-level people include local clergy, but also key lay leaders in the community, such as educators, journalists, politicians, lawyers, physicians, businesspeople, humanitarian aid workers, and other professionals who work with people. Finally, it is best if these persons come as individuals rather than as representatives of organizations, since this allows them to share more openly and not be restricted by a need to speak in the name of an institution.

GUIDELINES FOR AN EFFECTIVE DIALOGUE PROCESS

Traditional approaches to interfaith dialogue have often focused on involving the hierarchy and on producing official statements. Such has been the aim of interfaith dialogues in the former Yugoslavia that have been sponsored by organizations such as the Conference of European Churches, the Appeal of Conscience Foundation, and the World

Conference on Religion and Peace. In these high-level, official forums, the format has frequently been driven by the need for formal pronouncements. At times, this has meant that certain disputed topics are avoided, or that events become power contests between factions intent on controlling the outcome. In some cases, the process has also been dominated by lectures, panels, or debate procedures rather than by interaction that involves all participants. When these methodologies predominate, grievances tend to be either suppressed (when topics are avoided) or aggravated (in the context of debate). Space in which to rebuild fractured relationships must be given priority if interfaith dialogue can be expected to make any significant contribution to actually healing the wounds of war and reconciling seemingly incompatible differences between the parties.

Effectively guiding people of faith away from the entrapment of nationalist hostility in order for them to become agents of reconciliation requires both an identification with the suffering of their people and a challenge to discover the peacebuilding resources inherent within their faith traditions. Each of the Abrahamic traditions affirms the value of all human beings, the need to offer hospitality to the other, and the importance of self-examination as measures of faithfulness to God. However, in order to begin to facilitate transformation, interfaith dialogue must start with people's own experience. One must begin with people where they are, not where one might wish them to be. In the context of war, or postwar reconstruction, this means beginning with the experience of being a victim of aggression. Facilitators of effective interfaith dialogue must find creative ways to deal with everyone's sense of victimization. They must, then, help people from each religious community to examine together ways by which they can escape from the common tendency toward a cycle of revenge.

In the CSIS-sponsored seminars led by the author, the modus operandi has been storytelling. People need to share their suffering with one another across the ethno-religious divisions, even though it may seem divisive to give too much credence to complaints. When human beings, or whole societies, have been traumatized, they must be assured that their hurts are taken seriously by others. To be in solidarity with all sufferers does not mean that all suffering is equal. Nor does it mean that all groups are equally guilty. Such things are hardly ever equal. Furthermore, it does not mean accepting all the diagnoses, conclusions, perceptions, strategies, or positions of the sufferer. It does not entail agreeing with all the means by which the sufferer proposes that his or her hurts be redressed. Instead, it involves giving sensitive, compassionate attention to legitimate emotions of grief, fear, and anger. This requires the creation of "safe space," where one feels secure enough to reveal deep pain and to explore the redemptive possibilities in the wake of this sharing.

When people communicate their personal pain and reflect together on their common or different experience, they begin to build bonds. Yet, for people of faith, there can be more to this process than just sharing with one another. One can recount the traumatic experience with a sense of God's caring presence and unconditional acceptance. At a seminar in Bizovac, Croatia, in February 1995, a Croatian Baptist pastor, Bozidar Karlovic from Pakrac, shared his experience of being stabbed by Serbian troops. The anger was still audible in his voice as he showed us the scars on his body. Yet we also heard the testimony of faith in God that he gave to his attackers on that horrible day. When he asked them to ask God what they should do with him, it was not hard to believe that they stopped attacking him, not knowing what to make of his strength of spirit. His story was followed by that of Andjelko Sajlovic, a Serbian Orthodox priest from Kućanci. Father Sajlovic, who had lived in Croatian-controlled territory throughout the war in 1991, told of being shot three times by Croatian troops while taking his wife to the hospital one day. Again, this story was coupled with faith as this man of God later gave assurance of his forgiveness to one of the soldiers and invited him to turn to God. When asked what enabled him to respond with faith in the midst of such pain, he simply referred to his training in tranquility in a Serbian Orthodox monastery. The acceptance of these two people and their stories helped create an atmosphere of trust and hope that enabled others to then reveal their grief and pain.

This process of sharing one's suffering, and the strength coming from one's faith, has been repeated in more than thirty-five seminars during the past seven years. After participants have revealed these deep personal experiences, this author has found it helpful to point out that this catalytic process corresponds to the use of the lament motif in ancient Judaism. In the imprecatory Psalms, we find distressed people communicating their troubles to God, requesting God's protection, and recalling the ways in which God has previously been faithful. The purpose of such ritualization in ancient Israel was to offer up to God all suffering so that God could heal the pain and bring justice so that the individual could let go of the need for vindication. In response, participants have sometimes written their own laments, sharing them with the whole seminar as they offer up prayer to God. In each case, however, a challenge is extended to each religious community to utilize the great resources of their faith tradition to provide constructive avenues of expression for their people to mourn all their losses.

A similar process of storytelling can be used to help participants confront their fears of the future. People in the midst of war or postwar trauma are legitimately afraid of many things: personal safety, social transformation, economic crisis, political manipulation, and so on. Participants at a seminar titled "Coping with Calamity," held in Zavidovići, Bosnia, in April 1999, expressed many feelings of fear and uncertainty, including anxiety over war criminals going unpunished, collective guilt being indiscriminately applied to whole groups, creation of new national mythologies, loss of jobs, poverty, and a general sense of powerlessness. Furthermore, despite tremendous disagreements between Serbs and non-Serbs over the ongoing NATO bombing campaign in Yugoslavia, they all expressed great fear over the possible return of war to Bosnia-Herzegovina. People of faith can deal constructively with all these fears by also turning them over to God, a response demonstrated by participants in various seminars. At a seminar in Visoko, Bosnia, at the very end of the war in October 1995, Jagoda Bašajić, a Bosnian Croat woman, recounted her experience of spending time, with her children, in a Croatian concentration camp because she was married to a Muslim man. She closed the story by saying that it was her belief in God that had helped her to control the fear when she was tortured or used as a human shield.

The next stage in interfaith dialogue involves the identification of basic human needs, such as recognition, well-being, security, identity, community, and control over one's life. When communication has been severed, because of either war or the isolation caused by permanent ethnic cleansing, it is difficult for even well-intentioned people to understand the needs of the other. The media and the political leadership have frequently used propaganda to create misinformation and false rumor. It is important, however, that each group come to the point at which it can admit that the actions of even the worst enemy are motivated by very human needs and by fears that these needs will not be met. Basic needs are distinct from the positions someone takes on an issue in dispute. While a group's demands may be questionable, it is always important to express solidarity with basic interests as well as any legitimate pursuit of them. Fear that essential needs will be ignored frequently creates the kind of desperation that leads to intransigence and violence. By contrast, identifying common and compatible needs can help to create understanding and openness between adversaries. During a seminar in besieged Sarajevo in April 1995, an imam from Žepa, Hodžić Dervišalija, shared how he began to honestly ask himself about the needs of Serbs who were shooting at his Muslim people. Even though his own people were struggling to survive, he began to remember times in history when it was the Serbian people who had suffered at the hands of Muslims and concluded that both people were struggling to satisfy the same basic need for survival. This Muslim man was still angry over what had happened to his people during this war. He still viewed the act of aggression against his people as evil. But the aggressor was now rehumanized. As this courageous man recognized, in front of Serbian, Croatian, and Muslim participants, that the Serbian enemy had legitimate needs, the door was further opened for creative dialogue on the problems currently facing the ethnically mixed residents of Sarajevo.

One way of helping people to identify the needs of others is to invite them to participate in a perception clarification exercise. If people are asked to step into the shoes of another group and identify its values, concerns, fears, or intentions, they come to know how much or how little they understand each other and are, consequently, better able to work together to solve problems. The value of this kind of exercise was seen during a seminar in Bugojno, Bosnia-Herzegovina, in September 1999. Catholic and Muslim participants experienced significant conflict over what approach to take in overcoming ongoing problems caused by rampant nationalism, infused with a sense of victimhood. The Catholic Croats emphasized the need for forgiveness as an essential mind-set that could alter perspectives and behavior patterns. The Muslims, however, emphasized justice as a necessary requisite to any meaningful reconciliation. Arguments over these approaches were interjected into any topics discussed. The perception clarification exercise effectively helped each group to develop a better understanding of the other. People began to feel heard, and needs underlying each group's behavior were identified and affirmed as valid. Through this process, the Muslims began to assess a Catholic understanding of forgiveness, identifying aspects of it that they could affirm. As a result, Catholics began to realize that Muslims did not want to have their actions controlled by bitterness and hatred any more than did Catholics. In addition, Catholics began to examine the Muslim concern for justice, affirming that this also had a central place in Catholic theology. Together, the two groups affirmed a definition of justice that was broader than merely the rendering of punishment. The following day, Catholics voluntarily spoke about the lack of justice given to non-Croats in Croatian-controlled areas and Muslims spoke of their failure to forgive.

Acknowledgment of wrongdoing, or of holding wrong attitudes, is another essential step in constructive interfaith dialogue. If participants can acknowledge one another's pain, then they can also be helped to see that someone should be held responsible for inflicting the pain. In a two-sided conflict, for example, when the pain is experienced by people in the other group, then those responsible are likely to be from one's own group. The Jewish Scriptures are also helpful in opening the eyes of the victim to this reality. In the Old Testament prophets, the lament motif is paralleled by a call for confession of sin. Jeremiah, for example, identifies the suffering of his own people, but he also asks them to examine themselves and the Israelite people as a whole. The Old Testament prophets implore the people to ask God for salvation from their own sin and to remember God's forgiveness offered to both them and the enemy. People from war-ravaged societies in the former Yugoslavia easily identify with the losses suffered by the Jewish exiles of Jeremiah's time—loss of country, language, Temple—all the normal identity markers of their society. Yet they have also responded positively to the challenge of Jeremiah to examine the condition of their own hearts, and the actions of their own ethnic group, as a part of God's healing process. This author has seen courageous people from all the faith communities in this region begin to examine themselves. There is the Bosnian Franciscan, detained and almost killed by Serbian soldiers, who confessed the grudge he held against all Serbs and asked Serbian seminar participants to forgive the bitterness he had harbored against them. There is the Serbian Orthodox priest who admitted the complicity of his own church in the rise of Serbian nationalism and its contribution to the atmosphere that led to war in Bosnia-Herzegovina. Many times, in seminars, adversary ethnic groups have shared lists of atrocities that they know that "their" group committed against "the other."

Acknowledgment of wrongdoing is difficult to practice in situations of deep-seated conflict. When the sins committed *against* one's own people seem to far outweigh those committed *by* one's people, it is hard to be the first to admit anything. Recognition of one's own need for another's acknowledgment may sometimes help a very hurt person to overcome internal obstacles to the confession of sin. But whatever the rationale, honesty requires admitting that guilt is not entirely one-sided. All sides do share some responsibility for what has happened, even if unequally. At the same time, it is important to clarify for participants that there is a difference between personal confession of sin and acknowledgment of the wrongdoing by others in one's group. One should not take on personal responsibility for the sins of others.

Forgiveness is another difficult process that interfaith dialogue needs to address. When interfaith dialogue raises this topic, it is important to clarify first what is meant by forgiveness. Forgiveness is not absolution. It is not an act that frees people from the consequences of their actions. Forgiveness is not done for the sake of the other person, the victimizer. Instead it is a process by which the victim endeavors to free himself from the bondage of revenge. Forgiveness can be defined as giving up all hope of a better past. It is an act by which the victim moves out of the grip of the past and into an open and promising future. When approaching this topic during interfaith seminars, this author has found it useful to begin by asking people to recount times they have received forgiveness and then move on to times when they have offered it. Finally, it is important to ask people what has made it difficult to forgive. At a seminar in Priština, Kosovo, in July 2001, participants noted numerous reasons why forgiveness was difficult. Some of the factors they named included degree of isolation, stereotyping, vulnerability, hurt, sense of betrayal, lack of apology, group pressure, an attitude of arrogance on the part of the victimizer, and fear of repetition of the hurtful event. At the same time, participants suggested that focusing on others' needs and understanding their reasons for their action helped to nourish a sense of caring that could lead one to be more able to forgive. In the end, we need to allow people to approach this sensitive topic at their own speed, encouraging them along the way. One young Croatian woman, when introducing herself at a seminar in Osijek in June 1998, said she would never be able to forgive the Serbs for what they had done. At the end of the two-day event, she shared that she still could not forgive but that she knew that one day she would be able to do so. This movement represented great progress in her life and, if it could be replicated in the lives of other people, could contribute significantly toward the change in attitude necessary to reintegrate Serbs into Croatian society.

The discussion of justice concerns rightly brings the focus back from the individual to the society. If someone has been able to acknowledge the wrongs committed by his own group, and enter into a forgiveness that truly frees him from the victimhood syndrome, he is better able to explore the full picture of justice. A complete vision of justice will go much beyond the need for punishment, which is only one aspect of justice. Justice in all its fullness will be seen as the restoration of right relationships between people. It will involve coming together with other individuals from all ethnic groups in order to examine all the needs of all the people in the society. This inclusive picture of justice is positive in focus, not negative. It envisions a society in which the needs of victims, as well as perpetrators and indeed the whole community, are taken seriously. There is no longer an attempt to delegitimize some needs because the person or group is deemed unworthy. Yet there must still be some selection process among the various justice concerns. Meeting all the needs of any society is unrealistic. Achieving perfect justice is always a utopian ideal. One way to determine a strategy for an operative justice is to select the most basic level of need that has been thwarted at that moment in time in a given society, and to ask how this group of people might work together to address the obstacles that block its fulfillment.

At a recent seminar in Stubićke Toplice, Croatia, a local planning committee (composed of former seminar participants) preselected a justice concern that they believed was of central importance in Croatia today, namely, the treatment of minorities. The whole seminar then focused on identifying the needs of all parties, including Serbian refugees waiting to return, Bosnian Muslim refugees already there, and the majority Croatian population. At the beginning of the seminar, much time was spent assessing values that the various communities had in common. Based on these shared values, participants then drew up lists of basic human rights, community needs, and responsibilities. Numerous mutual concerns emerged, including respect for identity and culture, equality of education, and equal treatment by the law and government. The participants then divided into working groups to brainstorm creative projects that religious communities might pursue in order to help meet these needs. A variety of specific project proposals emerged, with specific participants volunteering to assist in implementing certain ones. The list of feasible ideas ranged from direct involvement with secular institutions (e.g., developing a contract with Croatian Television to do a documentary program on the plight of minorities, development of a truth and reconciliation commission, monitoring and reporting on violations of minority laws, promoting a better representation of minorities among police and judges, and encouraging national institutions to increase financial aid for refugee return and economic development) to empowerment of religious communities to address these concerns more powerfully (e.g., developing a Catholic journal that would include articles about minority problems, developing an e-mail list serve that would keep seminar participants informed about religious and cultural issues facing minority populations, and arranging for visits between the religious communities). Even if only a few of these ideas come to fruition, they will demonstrate the value of working over time with a committed core of people, building relationships so that people can trust one another enough to identify common needs and work together to help the process of resolving complex problems. This long-term, step-by-step process is much more likely to bring results than a highly publicized statement about minority rights made by a group of high-ranking religious officials.

ESSENTIAL FOLLOW-UP MEASURES

After seminars in which a brainstorming session has elicited possible future actions, participants should engage in effective follow-up. In the beginning years of the project directed by this author, this follow-up was not done adequately. For example, during the problem-solving seminar held in Fojnica, Bosnia-Herzegovina, in May 1996, a group of Catholic and Muslim religious people met together in a working group to discuss how they might support the creation of a new water system that would serve both the Muslim community of Fojnica and the Croatian community of Kiseljak, two cities that had experienced great violence during the Muslim-Croat fighting in 1993–94. A U.S. NGO had promised money to build the new water system, provided the two communities could work together on the project. Owing to immense suspicion, the municipal leadership of these cities could not agree to share a water supply. One of the imams from this working group proposed that the religious leaders form a team that could mediate the conflict between municipal leaders, bringing benefit to both communities. Despite genuine interest in the idea, it was never implemented. The primary reason for this failure was the lack of local personnel with the time and expertise to effectively train and supervise these volunteers.

To succeed in implementing local projects, one needs to have a local presence on the ground. For internationally led projects, such as the one directed by this author, this has necessitated training local consultants to telephone seminar participants, develop ongoing relationships, organize meetings, and provide necessary resources for people interested in following up project ideas. Such efforts can begin on a very simple level. In Serbia, meetings of seminar alumni began simply as discussions over coffee. The purpose was simply to further develop relationships, not to focus on any particular project implementation. Gradually, this committed nucleus of people shifted their focus to the creation of an organizing committee that eventually spawned a new institution, the Inter-religious Center in Belgrade, an organization that now implements a variety of its own projects. A similar process took place in Bosnia-Herzegovina, where seminar alumni also began to meet simply to further develop their relationships. This group then evolved into an advisory board that established the Center for Religious Dialogue, with offices in Sarajevo and Banja Luka. Both of these institutions have now developed their own sets of project priorities in addition to functioning as cosponsors, with us, of further seminars.

WAYS TO BUILD SUPPORTIVE INSTITUTIONAL STRUCTURES

Both the Inter-religious Center (IRC) and the Center for Religious Dialogue (CRD) are small institutions with staff that have placed a high priority on building personal relationships and rapport with the various religious communities. The directors of both organizations, each of whom was a former consultant working for this author, have developed close personal and working relationships with key leaders in various religious communities in Serbia and Bosnia-Herzegovina, respectively. The CRD director, Vjeko Saje, helped to negotiate the creation of the Inter-religious Council of Bosnia-Herzegovina, an institution composed of the four religious leaders in the country. Furthermore, he developed enough trust, soon after the end of the war, with Metropolitan Nikolaj of the Serbian Orthodox Church that the metropolitan called upon Saje, despite his Catholic affiliation, to help transport him to various Serbian Orthodox churches in the Muslim-Croat Federation. In Serbia another Catholic, Marijana Ajzenkol, general secretary of the IRC, also gained the respect and support of the Serbian Orthodox Church through her friendship with one of the staff at the Patriarchate and through one bishop who had been supportive of the conflict resolution project.

Both Saje and Ajzenkol have spent an immense amount of time building relationships among the core group of interethnic, inter-religious founders of the institutions. Most of these people have been seminar alumni who have demonstrated their support of such dialogue events over many years. Thus, there was a high degree of shared vision and a high level of commitment among the people who formed the governing boards of these institutions.

In Serbia, this core group of people began to coalesce following a seminar in Valjevo in December 1997. For the first time, Muslim leaders from Novi Pazar had come to a seminar at the invitation of a Serbian Orthodox bishop, Bishop Lavrentije of Šabac-Valjevo. The warm welcome they received surprised them. As a result, they determined to continue to meet under the guidance of Ajzenkol. Orthodox priests from Šabac-Valjevo, together with Muslims from Sandzak and Catholics and Protestants from Belgrade and Vojvodina, formed a close-knit group that began to meet informally and discuss possible cooperative projects. The IRC was officially formed in April 2000. Today, it supports various interfaith initiatives, including a working group to help make repairs to the properties of various religious communities. One such project, already undertaken, involved the painting of a fence around a Catholic church. A second project included taking Orthodox theology students to Zagreb and Sarajevo for the purpose of dialogue with Catholic and Muslim counterparts in those cities. Similar projects have included a trip to the Taize Community in France and the hosting of the interfaith Pontanima Choir from Sarajevo at a concert in Belgrade. A third project involved the publication of a journal of religious essays, to which clergy and laity from all the faith communities contributed. The IRC now also leads seminars on its own. One such seminar on prayer was the impetus for the publication of the above-mentioned journal. Another seminar, on the topic of religious freedom, was recently held at a Serbian Orthodox monastery. As of this writing, the IRC has just completed its first year of work as a separate institution, independent of CSIS. Already it has demonstrated great competence to function as a self-sufficient organization.

In Bosnia-Herzegovina, the initial core group of supporters formed during the first seminar held in Sarajevo in 1995. Under very difficult circumstances, during the siege of Sarajevo, people from all three ethnic groups and from each of the religious communities braved the bombing, and the possible disapproval of their coethnics, to attend an interfaith event. As stronger support developed for the CSIS project in the Bosnian Serb Republic, and seminars were held along the main fault lines between the Muslim-Croat Federation and the Bosnian Serb Republic in 1998, this core group of supporters began to develop into an advisory board for the establishment of a new institution. With the strong support, finally, of Serbian Orthodox bishop Hrisistom of Bihać-Petrovac, and the willingness of Serbian Orthodox priests from the Bosnian Serb Republic to participate in the advisory board for the new organization, the CRD was officially registered as an NGO in the Muslim-Croat Federation in December 1998 and in the Bosnian Serb Republic in May 1999. Despite tensions that soon followed during NATO's bombing of Yugoslavia, the new institution has continued to cosponsor seminars with CSIS, including single-confessional ones that focused on identity issues for the Serbian Orthodox and Muslim communities, in October 2000 and April 2001, respectively. In addition, using only its own local staff, the CRD led a seminar on conflict resolution in March 2001 for Sarajevo Phoenix, a local women's organization. Having completed a three-year transition process, the CRD is now totally independent from CSIS.

These two organizations are examples of what can be accomplished by small indigenous efforts at institution building. Their relationships with the various religious hierarchies give them credibility within the entire religious community. At the same time, they are independent from any hierarchical structure. This aim was, in fact, made very clear to the religious hierarchy, especially in Bosnia-Herzegovina, at the time the institutions were created. At times there are still tensions. Serbian and non-Serbian members of the advisory board in Bosnia have had major disagreements. Certain bishops refuse to support the efforts of such interfaith organizations. However, the very existence of these new NGOs, as a forum for building relationships and a springboard for joint working projects, is a sign of hope.

6

Mitigation in Northern Ireland

A Strategy for Living in Peace
When Truth Claims Clash

Joseph Liechty

AFTER DECADES OF INTENSE AND VOLUMINOUS DISCUSSION of the causes of conflict in Northern Ireland, the role of religion is far from settled, whether in pub arguments or academic analysis. Regrettably, discussion in both spheres is too often poisoned at the source because it starts with a question like, Is the conflict *really* religious, or is it *actually* national (or political or something else)? thus implicitly or explicitly requiring an either/or choice between religion and other factors. The choice is unnecessary and absurd. The wrong question is most unlikely to yield correct answers, and so analysis that rejects the significance of religion on the grounds of either/or logic is marred by bad reasoning, gaping blind spots, or both.

An appropriate analysis of causes of conflict employs both/and reasoning, which allows it both to make connections between various factors and to examine individual factors without suggesting that others are irrelevant. Thus concerning the role of religion in conflict, we might fruitfully and appropriately ask questions like: Does religion matter? In what ways does it matter? How much does it matter?

That religion matters in Northern Ireland can hardly be gainsaid. The Christian churches are the oldest continuous institutions in Irish society; the churches traditionally backed particular and opposing political options, and consequences and remnants of such attachments still linger significantly. Furthermore, measured by participation in religious practice, Ireland, including Northern Ireland, is by far the most Christian place in Europe, although percentages are declining.

Religion matters in numerous ways, great and small, but for current purposes, just two examples will need to suffice. (1) For centuries, the churches have been the most powerful agents in the socializing process in Ireland, through their influence on home and family life, church and community life, and education. That is a diminishing influence, and yet it remains true that no other agent of socialization—except perhaps for television—is as powerful. Much of this socialization is entirely positive, and yet it was and is socialization into segregation, which is one of the ways the churches have fed conflict and which suggests one of their possible contributions to peace. (2) Sometimes straightforward theology matters. One significant element of Protestant opposition to the 1998 Belfast Agreement (also known as the Good Friday Agreement) was revulsion at the notion of unrepentant paramilitary killers walking the streets, and one significant root of and rationale for this revulsion, especially among conservative Protestants, was that such an arrangement is an immoral offense against a biblical understanding of justice. I spent a couple weeks prior to the referendum on the Belfast Agreement working with ECONI (Evangelical Contribution on Northern Ireland) to develop a publicity campaign offering alternative viewpoints, which were widely disseminated among conservative Protestants. As so often in Irish history and affairs, politics and religion are not neatly separable.

How much does religion matter? While the question is valid, in reality scholarship is nowhere near ready to give a mature answer. Probably the best we can do for now is to work within the kind of integrating, connecting framework proposed by thoughtful scholars such as the political scientist Seamus Dunn, director of the Centre for the Study of Conflict at the University of Ulster, Coleraine. Dunn argues that conflict in Northern Ireland is not a single problem—not even a single multifaceted problem. Rather, it is best understood as "a set of interlocked and confused problems. . . . So the sort of arcane debates that try to establish, for example, whether it is a religious problem, or an economic problem, or a social problem, or a political problem are thought to be pointless, since it is all of these, and others as well."[1]

From January 1995 through June 2000, as codirectors of the Moving Beyond Sectarianism project for the Irish School of Ecumenics, Cecelia Clegg and I worked with numerous groups in Northern Ireland determined to come to grips with the problem of sectarianism—meaning, in Irish usage, the tangle of problems, including segregation, domination, and violence, that arise from malign intersections of religion and politics.[2] Most of these groups were church related or religiously motivated, and the problem of contentious religious truth claims frequently arose. As group members dug deeper and deeper to search out the tangled roots of sectarianism, they observed the way that religion had at times caused, intensified, or complicated conflict, and someone was likely to ask, Can we make any truth claims at all, or do they always feed sectarianism? It was a potentially explosive moment, because some participants had likely entered the process with the fear that addressing sectarianism meant that they would be asked to take the unacceptable step of abandoning or relativizing basic convictions. The issue took on magnified significance because those most concerned about these issues tended to be theological (and often social and political) conservatives, who must embrace any reconciling movement that hopes to be truly effective. Truth claims can be dangerous was our consistent response, but the danger is potential, not inherent. In any case, much depends on how and for what reasons the truth claim is made.

What makes truth claims sectarian and how to make them in positive or at least nondestructive ways became significant themes for the Moving Beyond Sectarianism project. The concept of mitigation is one way of framing even extreme, nonnegotiable truth claims in a way that minimizes or eliminates destructive consequences. Developed in the interchurch context of Northern Ireland, mitigation may also have applications in interfaith situations.

In any conflict, a capacity for compromise is a vital skill. The points on which groups clash can be negotiated by giving a little here, taking a little there. People accept, however grudgingly, a degree of disappointment, perhaps even bitter disappointment, as the price of a degree of satisfaction. They give up things they desire and value as the necessary cost of peace. In the absence of some ability to compromise, conflict can be intractable.

Some ideas and commitments, however, may be effectively non-negotiable, beyond the reach of compromise. These beliefs are so funda-mental, an individual or a group believes, that they cannot be abandoned or even modified without damaging something essential to personal or communal integrity. Although many ideas can be held as nonnegotiable, religious ideas in particular have a tendency to become nonnegotiable, because people not only value them highly but also believe that these ideas are in some way, perhaps quite directly, God-given. Because of this, principled, radical unwillingness to negotiate has a high and honored place in some religions, including Christianity. Already in the late second or early third century, Tertullian famously observed what had been true from the beginning, that the blood of the martyrs—the ultimate in non-negotiators—is the seed of the church, and so it has remained through the centuries. This is one impulse Christianity inherited directly from Judaism, which from the beginning extolled uncompromising faith-fulness. From this perspective, some beliefs may be accepted or rejected, but they are not really up for negotiation.

While some people seem to treat every detail of their beliefs as nonnegotiable, even people with good compromising, negotiating skills may hold some beliefs or commitments that are nonnegotiable. In fact, most people probably have some nonnegotiable beliefs. They may never become aware of it, because circumstances never expose the beliefs as nonnegotiable, and, in any case, most nonnegotiable beliefs never become a source of conflict. When nonnegotiables do clash, however, they make a conflict vastly more difficult.

Conflicting nonnegotiables may be resolved in several ways. One possibility is that the nonnegotiability was only apparent—when pressed hard on the matter, a group discovers that it had falsely ele-vated this particular stance to the realm of the nonnegotiable, and com-promise is in fact possible, whether willingly or grudgingly. Or perhaps the stark clash of nonnegotiables takes both parties well past bitter compromise and allows them to see issues in a different light, where a new and superior synthesis or alternative emerges, to their mutual ben-efit. Another possibility is that a nonnegotiable core remains, but the process of negotiation reveals that certain accretions to that core can be stripped away without loss, and the reconfigured core no longer poses the difficulties it once did.

Yet another possibility, however, is that the apparently nonnegotiable will prove to be actually nonnegotiable. The group cannot alter or abandon this particular commitment without doing grave and unacceptable damage to its identity. Imagine, for example, a situation in which group A, a Christian group, is in conflict with group B, which adheres to another religion. A mediator between them identifies a crucial clash of core beliefs. "Group A," she says, "you have your ten commandments; group B happens to have seven commandments. In fact you share five of these commandments, and it is the ones you do not share that aggravate the conflict. Therefore, if you could both agree to keep the five commandments you share and abandon the remainder, this could be the shift that would make peace between you possible." From outside those groups, retaining most of one's beliefs and giving up a few for the sake of peace may seem like an honorable solution. But from inside, the issue is likely to look entirely different. These are not just any beliefs, people might think, and we did not make them up to suit ourselves so that we might now abandon them to suit ourselves; they were given to us by God, and we conform our lives to them. Abandoning these beliefs is too high a price for peace, because it is at the cost of our integrity, identity, and allegiance. Either there is another way to peace or there is no peace.

An actual and difficult example of nonnegotiability concerns the claims of the Abrahamic faiths, Islam, Judaism, and Christianity, each to be the exclusive way to salvation. In fact, some adherents of these faiths do negotiate the difficulties posed by exclusivity, principally by ignoring or rejecting it. Effectively they are saying, we are committed Muslims, Jews, or Christians, but we do not accept these particular exclusive tenets of our faith; we believe there are other ways to salvation. Some such capacity to negotiate may seem essential to create lasting peaceable relations among these three religions. It may appear that without a recognition by adherents of any faith that people from other faiths not only can be saved, but can be saved through the observance of their own faith, there cannot be peace among the religions and therefore there cannot be peace.

Certainly one approach to nonnegotiables that can have real integrity and good effect is to make them negotiable. No doubt much of what people regard as nonnegotiable should not be, and the best way of dealing with it is to demote it to the ranks of the negotiable. That strategy will not always work, however, and a good example is the exclusive claims of the monotheistic faiths. Making acceptance that believers from other faiths will be saved in and through their faiths a necessary condition of peace is likely to be a counsel of despair, because it will never be adhered to sufficiently to make peace. The problem is not that people hang on to exclusivity out of some bigoted, perverse desire to feel superior to others or even to sustain conflict. The problem is that these exclusive claims are deeply embedded in scriptures held to be of inestimable, God-given value. Therefore, attempts to neglect, deny, overturn, or substantially alter—or in any other way negotiate— what is plausibly held to be nonnegotiable cannot form a stable basis for peace, because such efforts will always inspire protest and reaction. The protest may be by a majority against an elite, a minority against a majority, one generation against the previous, but it will surely be made, and in every case the protesters will make a persuasive, powerful case that they are being faithful to the sacred tradition. Attempts to nego- tiate what faithful adherents reasonably believe to be nonnegotiable are likely to lead to the kind of split in the tradition, whether formal or informal, that will undercut the peacemaking benefits meant to follow from the negotiation.

Arguing that some beliefs with potentially damaging consequences simply cannot be negotiated successfully may sound like another counsel of despair. I do not mean it to be, although I recognize the gravity of the problem. Mitigation is the scheme I want to propose for dealing con- structively with situations where conflicting nonnegotiables lead to destructive consequences and yet cannot be compromised. By mitigation I mean the capacity to lessen or eliminate possible negative outcomes of a belief, commitment, or action—while still upholding it. What cannot be negotiated can sometimes be mitigated.

One fundamental distinction between negotiating and mitigating applies consistently. Negotiation works by rejecting, neglecting, or sub- stantially changing the perceived obstacle to peace, while mitigation maintains the problematic belief or practice but seeks to nullify destructive consequences.

The line between negotiation and mitigation is not always entirely clear, however. This is not surprising, because they are different means to the common end of peace. Therefore, a person or group desiring peace may practice both negotiation and mitigation, in tandem or at different times. The boundary between negotiating and mitigating is also blurred at times by the type of strategies employed. A consistent, if not quite constant, feature of mitigation is that it seeks to lessen destructive consequences arising from within a tradition by appealing to resources from that same tradition. The tradition works to heal the tradition.

Negotiation, by contrast, is much more likely to operate by external means. In fact, negotiation by external means is negotiation in its sharpest and most characteristic form. It works by applying, whether explicitly or implicitly, some principle of judgment that is external to and effectively higher than the tradition. External negotiation trumps tradition with an alternative. But negotiation, like mitigation, can also employ strategies and logic internal to the tradition. Internal negotiation is clearly negotiation, because a problematic belief is rejected rather than maintained. And yet the means to achieve this, as with mitigation, is an appeal to the tradition.

In the two practical examples that follow, a fuller discussion would deal with the options of external and especially internal negotiation, as well as with mitigation. For the sake of brevity, however, I will attend only to mitigation.

ONE BREAD, ONE BODY AND DOMINUS IESUS

Although neither of these recent Catholic Church documents is focused primarily on relationships with Protestants, both are useful in showing how the Catholic Church evaluates Protestantism and some of the tensions that arise from that assessment. *One Bread, One Body*, issued by the British and Irish Catholic bishops in 1998, is a teaching document on the Catholic doctrine and practice of the Eucharist.[3] In the way it handled excluding Protestants from sharing communion with Catholics in all but a handful of instances, the document had, we argue in *Moving Beyond*

Sectarianism, the sectarian consequences of hardening boundaries and overlooking Protestant concerns. *Dominus Iesus* was issued in August 2000 by the Vatican's Congregation for the Doctrine of the Faith. Only the Catholic Church, according to this document, is a fully Christian church. While the merits of the Protestant churches are recognized, they are not actually "Churches in the proper sense," but rather "ecclesial communities."[4] The potential sectarian implications in such a judgment are obvious.

As with most contentious issues, Catholics who disagree with these stances can take a negotiating stance, whether external or internal. But many Catholics will not wish or be able to deal with these issues by means of negotiation, even though they may share their negotiating brothers' and sisters' regret about sectarian consequences. Catholic teaching is a whole, they may reason, so Catholics are not free to pick and choose as they please. *One Bread, One Body* is a reiteration of traditional Catholic teaching on the Eucharist, and no doctrine and practice is more central to the life of the Catholic community. *Dominus Iesus* too simply reiterates traditional Catholic teaching on the ecclesial status of Protestantism—although some careful readers, both Catholic and Protestant, find in the document a less irenic approach to this problem than has been characteristic of the Catholic Church since the Second Vatican Council. Given the precedent for the teachings of *One Bread, One Body* and *Dominus Iesus,* some Catholics, probably many, will see no room for negotiation. They do not wish to give offense, but if sectarian consequences can be dealt with only by rejecting or ignoring these doctrines, then they cannot be dealt with.

In these circumstances, mitigation might take several forms. Concerning communion, one form is simply to be sensitive in anticipating and avoiding circumstances in which the practice of exclusive communion may give offense. Another approach might seek positive relationships with Protestants, including sharing worship in ways that are approved by Catholic teaching and that work around and do not draw attention to the problem of communion. A third, in this case drawing explicitly on the standards of the Catholic Church and all but indistinguishable from internal negotiation, is to consider the varieties of accepted practice concerning shared communion within the worldwide Catholic Church. In the same vein, mitigators might think through the content of various agreements the Catholic Church has reached with others on the subject of communion and test whether the implications of those agreements have been sufficiently put into practice. A mitigating spirit at least considers the question, Does the existing and accepted practice and teaching of the Catholic Church allow a degree of latitude concerning shared Eucharist that is not sufficiently explored in Ireland today? Concerning how Catholics should regard Protestant churches, mitigation will involve a question of proportion. The negative judgment of Protestant churches as merely ecclesial communities rather than as full and proper churches will be maintained, but it will be accompanied by full awareness of the genuine merit of Protestant expressions of faith, of the way God has used Protestant churches as instruments of salvation, and of all that Catholics have to learn from Protestants. Since the Second Vatican Council, such mitigating stances have characterized formal Catholic teaching on Protestantism. How far Catholics have lived it out in relation to Protestants has varied, of course, from time to time and place to place.

ANTI-CATHOLICISM

A second issue is the anti-Catholicism of the Protestant tradition. The traditional stance of the Protestant mainstream, enshrined in doctrinal statements by the Church of Ireland (the Thirty-Nine Articles) and Presbyterianism (the Westminster Confession) and in much rhetoric and practice by Methodism, might be characterized as believing that the teachings and practice of the Catholic Church are so radically in error that it cannot be accepted as a Christian church, or at least that the Catholic Church is a deficient and lesser church. It is essentially the mirror image of the traditional Catholic judgment of Protestantism.

For the most part, Protestant mainstream churches have altered their stance toward Catholicism by means that amount to internal negotiation. Negotiating anti-Catholicism—whether by internal or external means—will not be an acceptable option for everyone, however. For some people, the old Protestant critique of Catholicism continues to maintain its integrity and authority. What has seemed to some other

Protestants, including some conservatives, a legitimate and necessary internal negotiation—that is, changing attitudes to Catholicism for reasons of faithfulness to the gospel message—will seem to nonnegotiators to be straightforward external negotiation and as such contemptible—abandoning the gospel in order to embrace a position more in step with modernity.

For those who cannot negotiate, the only way to meet the moral imperative to address the sectarian implications of anti-Catholicism will be mitigation. Of the mitigating resources available within conservative Protestantism, I will mention just two. The first is a distinction between religious separation and social separation. As several fundamentalists told us, what their critique of Catholicism requires of them is religious separation, expressed chiefly in objecting to and avoiding shared worship. But social separation need not follow. The distinction allows at least positive neighborly relations and, potentially, cooperation in various enterprises without a religious element.

Over the past twenty years, evangelical attitudes toward Catholics have changed significantly, and the Northern Ireland politico-religious landscape looks significantly different for it. Sometimes the evangelicals involved have found evangelical reasons for negotiating anti-Catholicism. Other evangelicals, however, have essentially retained the old Protestant critique of Catholicism, but, acting on their freedom to relate to and work with Catholics outside the explicitly religious sphere, they have been involved in some important cross-community initiatives with Catholics. It is a stance that puts those who take it in awkward and difficult circumstances at times, but it also opens up creative opportunities for mitigating the sectarian implications of anti-Catholicism, and therefore for peace in Northern Ireland, through positive relationships and shared work.

Among Protestants, negotiation of any sort is least likely to be an option for the Orange Order, the still powerful conservative Protestant politico-religious organization probably best known internationally for its annual parades, some of which become flashpoints of sectarian contention every summer. Nonetheless, the Order will have available to it the mitigating principle of distinguishing between religious and social separation, as well as another principle that is particular to one of the Order's core documents, "The Qualifications of an Orangeman." "Qualifications" begins with an exhortation to Christian commitment and practice and then moves on to detail the Orangeman's stance toward Catholicism.

> [H]e should strenuously oppose the fatal errors of the Church of Rome, and scrupulously avoid countenancing (by his presence or otherwise) any act or ceremony of Popish Worship; he should by all lawful means resist the ascendancy of that Church, its encroachments and the extension of its power.[5]

Anti-Catholicism, then, is a nonnegotiable woven into the very fabric of Orangeism, along with the potential for destructive and sectarian consequences that follow from it. "Qualifications" proceeds without a break, however, to put forward a mitigating principle: the Orangeman is to maintain this stance toward Catholicism while at the same time "ever abstaining from all uncharitable words, actions or sentiments towards his Roman Catholic brethren."[6] Abstaining from uncharity may be a weak version of the command for Christians to love their neighbors, but it is a recognizable version. It is also a potential mitigating principle to apply to words and actions with sectarian implications or consequences. The very possibility may strain the credulity of many outside the Order, but the logic behind this passage does serve a mitigating function at times.

In many cases, then, as in the two described briefly, what cannot be negotiated can in some way be mitigated. Indeed, read by any Christian with a mitigating desire and spirit, the Bible, and especially the teaching and example of Jesus, reveals itself as a treasury of mitigating principles. If I were to choose a bottom line from among the many mitigating principles to be drawn from the Bible, I would probably cite Jesus' command to "love your enemies and pray for those who persecute you" (Matt. 5:44, NRSV). As a mitigating principle, this is as tough-minded as it is idealistic. It simply assumes that Christians will have enemies, and the idea that enemies may be dealt with by negotiating the points of contention is not entertained. It is framed in clear and simple terms, and positioned in the center of faith; Jesus' followers are to live like this, he says, "so that you may be children of your Father in heaven" (Matt. 5:45, NRSV), who loves in just this way. It is set in a context that makes it clear that loving enemies is about behavior as much as attitude.

As a mitigating principle, it is entirely incompatible with doing harm to opponents and calls for much more.

For any reader of even a slightly skeptical bent, however, citing the resources in Christianity for mitigating may be significant chiefly for exposing the too common and sometimes spectacular failure of Christians to use these resources. Walter Wink summarizes two thousand years of Christian thought and practice concerning a biblical text on love of enemies by saying, "Christians have, on the whole, simply ignored this teaching."[7] Without a mitigating spirit, mitigating principles are a dead letter. Unpracticed, they are more a chastisement and embarrassment than a resource.

The existence of that mitigating spirit in Northern Ireland can seem tenuous. At times, an exacerbating spirit is much more noticeable. It is important to recognize and honor, however, the presence in Northern Ireland of a mitigating spirit, which operates in a way that provides a welcome exception to Wink's judgment that Christians have largely ignored biblical teaching on loving enemies. Forgiveness is always a form of love, and practiced in hard cases it is specifically the love of enemies. Forgiveness is also a gospel value that seems to have penetrated Irish Christianity in its many forms, and to profound effect. While the public significance of forgiving those who have wronged one's own people has been most apparent in a few high-profile cases during the violence of Northern Ireland's "Troubles," the widespread practice of forgiveness, by Christians and others, in its most basic form—renouncing retaliation—has surely been of inestimable value in keeping the death rate relatively low and maintaining a relatively intact society. Keeping conflict in Northern Ireland in a proper perspective must include recognizing how much worse it could have been. The practice of forgiveness has been an important form of mitigation.

Whatever the state of past and present practice, mitigation is a mix of skills, habits, and mind-set that is accessible to everyone. In every situation, but especially a situation of endemic conflict, mitigation is also an obligation on everyone who has any pretensions to being a person of goodwill. From radical and conservative perspectives alike, reconciliation is sometimes criticized as the compromising, negotiating enemy of justice and truth. The criticism is that fear of giving offense will prevent the rightly and necessarily offensive truth from being spoken, that reconciliation operates in the spirit of crying peace where there is no peace. The practice of mitigation—by recognizing the integrity and necessity of making truth claims and setting some boundaries on how it is done—simultaneously answers the criticism and returns the scrutiny to those who make truth claims. If those pursuing truth claims are genuinely concerned with the truth, then they may not fear to give offense, but they will take no pleasure in it, and they will certainly fear giving needless offense, which can only harm the cause of truth. Where truth is pursued without regard for destructive consequences, it calls into question whether the pursuers' commitment is really to the truth or to some other cause, in which truth claims are merely weapons. Mitigation is both a tool for making truth claims in a constructive way and a standard of judgment for assessing the integrity of those making truth claims.

NOTES

1. Seamus Dunn, "The Conflict as a Set of Problems," in *Facets of the Conflict in Northern Ireland*, ed. Seamus Dunn (Basingstoke, U.K.: Macmillan, 1995), 7–8.

2. Many ideas touched on in passing in this chapter, as in the case of this definition of sectarianism, are dealt with at length in Joseph Liechty and Cecelia Clegg, *Moving Beyond Sectarianism: Religion, Conflict, and Reconciliation in Northern Ireland* (Blackrock, County Dublin: Columba Press, 2001).

3. The Catholic Bishops' Conferences of Ireland, Scotland, England, and Wales, *One Bread, One Body: A Teaching Document on the Eucharist in the Life of the Church, and the Establishment of General Norms on Sacramental Sharing* (Dublin: Veritas Publications, 1998).

4. Congregation for the Doctrine of the Faith, "Declaration—*Dominus Iesus:* On the Unicity and Salvific Universality of Jesus Christ and the Church." Available on-line at www.vatican.va/roman_curia/congregations/cfaith/documents/rc_con_cfaith_doc_20000806_dominus-iesus_en.html (April 4, 2001).

5. Quoted in Kevin Haddick-Flynn, *Orangeism: The Making of a Tradition* (Dublin: Wolfhound Press, 1999), 381–382.

6. Ibid., 382. Some versions of the "Qualifications" use the wording "towards Roman Catholics" rather than "towards his Roman Catholic brethren."

7. Walter Wink, *Engaging the Powers* (Minneapolis: Fortress Press, 1992), 175.

Part III

Peacebuilding through Interfaith Organizations

7
Religion and Interfaith Conflict
Appeal of Conscience Foundation

Arthur Schneier

*I*N THIS ERA OF INSTANT COMMUNICATION, when we learn about events in distant places in almost real time, we have become increasingly aware of conflicts that appear to have religious overtones or that even appear to have been prompted and exacerbated by religious differences. The tragic consequences of the recent wars in the Balkans are perhaps the most graphic examples of such events, but this is only one region of many that have experienced genocidal killing in recent times. When we look for the causes of such conflicts we find a variety of reasons, some of them economic or political, some ethnic, even tribal, and some cultural, but we find that there is one constant that seems to have an overriding importance. That constant is a religious difference that somehow has become paramount in the minds of those involved and for them justifies their inflamed passions and heightened brutality. To the outside observer, those conflicts take on the character of religious wars and are often characterized as such by the media.

No religion today condones genocide or brutality. We at the Appeal of Conscience Foundation (ACF) and I personally have devoted our energies for the past thirty-five years on behalf of religious freedom, human rights, and what I firmly believe in, the idea of "live and let live." In working with religious leaders in conflicts, I have found that in every case those leaders agree with me and condemn all brutal actions taken by members of their faith.

There is no doubt that the twentieth century was the bloodiest century in the history of civilization. Blood was shed at times in the name of God and righteousness. Blood was shed over religious and ethnic issues—conflicts not easily resolved. But, with my colleagues who have inscribed this phrase into their hearts, I believe that "a crime committed in the name of religion is the greatest crime against religion." It is essential that the Cross, the Crescent, and the Star of David become symbols of peace, tolerance, and mutual respect.

NEW APPROACHES TO INTERFAITH DIALOGUE

I believe that interfaith dialogue in zones of conflict can best be accomplished through the good offices of a neutral third party. The ACF, which has worked to improve religious and human rights in many areas of the world, is such a neutral third party. It is a U.S. organization I founded in 1965 that has reached out to include leaders of many religions, as well as leaders in business and other lay professions. It is ecumenical in the sense that it adheres to the principle that all religions have an equal right to exist. It is precisely because it is an organization anchored by religion, with members who are high-ranking clergy representing the Catholic, Protestant, Orthodox, Jewish, and Muslim faiths who in conflicts do not favor one side or the other, that the ACF provides the temporizing influence of a neutral third party. "It is," as I stated in my remarks to the Organization for Security and Cooperation in Europe (OSCE) in early 2001, "the role that religious leaders can and must play to reduce strife, advance tolerance, and build a society based on the rule of law."

It is those credentials that allow the ACF to initiate discussions among religious leaders in zones of conflict. We have found that to maximize the effectiveness of such discussions, it is most important, especially in the beginning, to have meetings with religious leaders in their own country. Frequently, strong feelings of nationalism by some in the religious hierarchy can present barriers. That is particularly true in countries where religion and nationality have been closely interwoven throughout history. Russia is one such example, Serbia another. In such instances it becomes important to identify supporters of interfaith dialogue within the hierarchy, to strengthen the case for interfaith interaction, and to isolate those whose nationalistic opinions, often couched in religious terminology, would lead to increasingly greater confrontation. In spite of the trend toward globalization, the pull backward toward tribalization and fragmentation of society is strong and needs to be addressed.

To have a better chance of success at resolving interfaith conflicts, which usually bring with them strong, sometimes violent, emotions, it is important to involve the concerned country's government and seek its support. Further, the ACF has consistently sought to involve leading government officials in those countries where conferences were scheduled to take place. The participation of such high-ranking officials gives the conference stature and political weight, which allows the conference participants to feel that they are being taken seriously and that their interests are important to others. In every instance when the ACF planned to hold a conference of religious leaders to discuss national issues, whether within their country or in some other venue, involved national governments such as Russia, Serbia, Bosnia, Croatia, and Turkey were kept informed and sometimes participated in the deliberations. In every instance their involvement was crucial to a successful outcome. In addition, the U.S. Department of State, the United Nations, the OSCE, the European Union, and world religious organizations were always kept informed.

BRINGING INTERFAITH DIALOGUE
TO A CONFLICT SITUATION

In many instances interfaith conflict is rooted in age-old folk sayings that are handed down from generation to generation. In the work that the ACF accomplished in the former Yugoslavia, for example, these very problems had to be overcome before any progress could be made. During the first conference that was organized by the ACF, in Berne, Switzerland, in November 1992, to deal with the conflict in Bosnia, the first day of the conference was replete with recriminations detailing brutalities ostensibly perpetrated by one or the other religion's adherents. Orthodox, Catholic, and Muslim leaders went back even further into history to prove their contention that the other side was more savage in its attacks.

Despite the blame they were placing on one another for the bloody events, which in any other conference context would have been interpreted as a sign of failure, that exchange was actually cathartic for all sides. Although Muslims, Orthodox, and Catholics lived side by side in the former Yugoslavia and its predecessor states, there had never been a meeting of all the top leaders of the three religious communities until they sat at the same table at the 1992 conference. Theirs is a society that often considers retribution to be the only way to deal with problems of intolerance. The accusations the three made against one another were helpful because in the past, before contact at the leadership level, the three religions had heard only their respective side of atrocities perpetrated by the members of another religion. For the first time, all sides were heard and noted.

The issue that we confronted at that time was the war that was then raging in Bosnia, between Serbs, who wanted to join Serbia and split Bosnia into areas defined along ethnic lines, and Bosnians, who wanted to retain the country as it was. In that conflict were also Croats, who were not as concentrated in definable areas, who sometimes sided with Bosnians but often fought against them, and who opposed Serbs but also wanted a slice of Bosnia to be joined to Croatia.

Our position was that it was vital for the success of the conference to follow what the international community had supported through the United Nations, the OSCE, and the European Union. Our contention was that the fighting had to stop, that the people of Bosnia needed to cooperate with one another, and, most important for our immediate purposes, that the three major religions of Bosnia had to continue the contact established at the conference table, denounce the hate-mongering rhetoric, and cooperate with one another to bring relief to all who were suffering in Bosnia, without regard to religious affiliation. Those were difficult goals to achieve, and we had no illusions that one conference of religious leaders would be able to sweep away many generations of distrust and hate. At the same time, we felt strongly that some headway had been made. These religious leaders, upon returning to their homes, were certain to bring fresh ideas of moderation to their faithful. The strong declaration demanding an end to the killing, which they all signed, was a signal document, for the first time demonstrating that cooperation among the religious communities in the former Yugoslavia was possible.

After the conference ended the ACF kept in touch with all the participants. We attempted to build on the conference declaration, but we soon recognized that cooperation among the religions had not yet advanced beyond the stage of rhetoric and that another attempt at religious cooperation was necessary. The killing in Bosnia did not stop and, despite the best efforts by all involved, the religious leaders were still not cooperating successfully anywhere in the former Yugoslavia. For that reason, the ACF organized the Bosphorus Conference in February 1994, this time in Istanbul, with the cooperation and cosponsorship of Patriarch Bartholomew I and the Ecumenical Patriarchate. This conference sought broader participation, taking in other Balkan countries, Central Asian countries, Russia, and Turkey. Our goal here was the same as that in the first conference, to bring about close or closer cooperation among the religions in those areas where there were conflicts.

However, later it became clear that issues dealing with other countries could not be resolved easily in the context of a multinational conference. From analysis of the Bosphorus Conference, we saw that the reason it provided only partial success was that the issues addressed were too diffuse, and that, because of the geographical spread from the Balkans to Central Asia, we lost the sharp focus that is required to make a strong impact. Therefore, the next year, in March 1995, we organized the Conflict Resolution Conference in Vienna, which was a great deal more effective. It was immediately apparent that there was a more cordial relationship among the religious leaders, which had emerged as a result of our previous conferences. This conference focused strictly on the Bosnian conflict and initiated the organization of an interreligious council for Bosnia-Herzegovina that the local leaders of the Orthodox, Muslim, Catholic, and Jewish communities joined.

The 1995 Appeal of Conscience Conflict Resolution Conference in Vienna predated the Dayton Peace Accords, which were the instrument that ended the Bosnian conflict. Basically, the declaration that was signed by the religious leaders who were present in Vienna was very similar in tone to Dayton and very likely could have influenced the negotiators in Dayton, who, of course, were in contact with the religious leaderships of their countries. As a follow-up to those conferences in May 1998, the ACF hosted in the United States the Inter-Religious Council of Bosnia-Herzegovina in order to bolster its members' resolve to stand together and preach tolerance and cooperation to the faithful, in individual as well as in joint appearances in their home country.

WHEN CONFLICTS LOOK HOPELESS

In March 1999 the Appeal of Conscience Foundation organized another conference in Vienna, this time on Kosovo. We recognized that this conference would not be like the others, because Kosovo was not an independent country but rather an integral part of Serbia that Serbs considered a vital link to their history and national culture. Emotions among Serbs ran high about Kosovo, and the Yugoslav federal authorities exacerbated the situation by putting stronger pressure on the majority Albanian population through repression and persecution. The worst came with the introduction of special police and military forces to pursue a brutal policy of ethnic cleansing. Albanians, who had been the majority in Kosovo for generations, were being driven out systematically, their homes and places of worship were being destroyed, and many were killed indiscriminately. The Albanians were first seeking educational opportunities and recognition of their language and traditions. When these opportunities and cultural recognition were not forthcoming, their petition later hardened into a demand for autonomy and, for some, independence.

It was against that background that the ACF began the laborious task of contacting Muslim, Orthodox, and Catholic leaders in Kosovo and inviting them to participate in a conference that had as its aim the cooperation of the three religions to help bring about an end to the killing and initiate an atmosphere that allowed for cooperation. There was suspicion on all sides. Finally, however, despite considerable danger, particularly for the Muslim delegates at border crossings, all three religions sent their representatives to Vienna to discuss the issues. In this instance, as well, it was the first time that the Orthodox bishop of Kosovo, the Catholic bishop of Kosovo, and a leading Muslim from Kosovo had met. Once again, recriminations of past wrongs were voiced at the beginning of the discussion. Although there was considerable hesitation, and the delegates from the three religions had differing views on many issues, they were able to come to agreement in the Vienna declaration, entitled "Kosovo Peace and Tolerance," on the most important issues: to "stop the killing" and "end the polemics of hate"; to "permit all to worship and work in the knowledge that their basic human rights will not be violated"; to "preserve houses of worship . . . of all faiths"; and to "permit all ethnic and religious communities to retain their cultural and linguistic heritage."

Although the religious leaders agreed that the killing had to stop in Kosovo, the political leaders who were meeting in France at the same time could not reach agreement on the issues before them. The killing continued and almost immediately brought on the NATO air war that led to the withdrawal of Yugoslav forces from Kosovo, in effect making Kosovo a UN protectorate. However, as strife in Kosovo abated because of NATO's involvement, neighboring Macedonia, which has a large Albanian minority, began to experience ethnic conflict. This spillover from Kosovo lends credence to the belief that we must continue to encourage religious leaderships in the region to work toward the goal of ethnic and religious tolerance for all. Tolerance cannot stop at national boundaries; it must extend to neighboring multiethnic and multireligious areas, where identical cultural differences often exist and conflicts can arise and lead to further bloodshed.

THE LIMITATIONS OF RELIGIONS IN INFLUENCING EVENTS

These events, particularly those in Kosovo, underline dramatically the limitations that religions and their leaders face in making peace. It is not they who control the military forces and it is not they who make the political decisions. Therefore, they can influence the quest for peace only when there is a political will to have peace. That is not to say that they should not be forceful in their demand to stop ethnic and interfaith violence as it occurs, as was the case with the Orthodox bishop of Kosovo, who was adamantly opposed to the brutalities of ethnic cleansing committed against Albanians; such demands are fully concomitant with all religions. But it is only after peace is achieved that religious leaderships can help bring about an atmosphere for cooperation and tolerance.

HOW RELIGIONS CAN CONTRIBUTE TO PEACE

The most important contribution religions can make to peace is to recognize that when conflict emerges, they have the responsibility to speak out against violence and persecution. In our era religion is not the cause of conflict, although it is often used as the excuse. No religion supports such policies, and today's interfaith conflicts have roots that are nonreligious. They could stem from cultural, economic, linguistic, or other sources. However, religion, unfortunately, is often the most visible difference between contesting groups and, as a result, frequently is blamed for conflicts. When such conflicts arise, it becomes paramount that voices be heard that characterize the conflict for what it is and distance religion from it, as well as promote compassionate understanding and tolerance. It is imperative, if we are to have greater tolerance and understanding among religious and ethnic groups during periods of stress and trauma, that outside ecumenical organizations, such as the ACF, as well as organizations that represent individual religions, provide avenues for dialogue between people of differing faiths. The barometer of emerging democracies is how the majority treats the minority.

When conflicting sides have come to the same table to try to discuss the issues that divide them, it is important to quickly find points of agreement. One issue that all religions have accepted is that religious sites, whether they are houses of worship or monuments, are a part of the precious heritage of culture and civilization. As such they must be protected from destruction. Recalling the destruction of my synagogue in Vienna on Kristallnacht, November 10, 1938, I am horrified by the desecration of any religious site. It is an onslaught on one's identity and heritage that leads to dehumanization and the destruction of human beings. To bring even greater attention to this core issue, I asked my

Christian and Muslim colleagues to join me in an appeal to the United Nations to call on member-states to "stop the desecration of holy sites" in December 2000. That appeal provides a useful beginning for any discussion of interfaith conflict, concerning an issue that all, with the exception of the Taliban in Afghanistan, can agree on. That appeal was sponsored as a resolution by 118 nations in the United Nations General Assembly and adopted by consensus on May 31, 2001. The resolution condemns all acts of violence against religious sites and calls on all states to exert their utmost efforts to ensure that religious sites are fully respected and protected.

Another effective means for cooperation among religions is an interfaith council. Such an ecumenical religious organization can have a lasting effect on the relationship among the religions. It can address and try to resolve problems within the religious communities before they become critical and before anger leads to violence.

The Appeal of Conscience Foundation has also emphasized the use of electronic media to bring the message of cooperation home to a larger audience. In the past we encouraged the scheduling of radio programs in which all religious leaders in the country would participate, to bring the message of cooperation and tolerance to their faithful. To some degree, that worked in Bosnia. There could be radio programs in which religious leaders participate together, as well as appearances of individual leaders of each religion, to explain to their faithful the need for tolerance and cooperation. Television can also be used for the same purpose, but it is more expensive and more difficult to organize. Joint news conferences dealing with local events are another means to indicate cooperation, unity, and tolerance for other religions.

We further believe that the young clergy in areas of interfaith conflict should have the opportunity to visit countries that have harmonious relations among their ethnic and religious communities. Such visits would allow the clerics to see what innovations could be used within their own countries to improve interfaith relations, bring greater stability, and maintain peace.

Those are some of the concepts we have used to bring about greater tolerance and temporize the violence in interfaith conflicts. We believe that those concepts are universal and, with some adjustment, can be applied in any situation where religions appear to collide. At the same time we also know that religious leaders cannot stop wars or bring about solutions to problems that have no basis in religion but are ruled by other forces. It is the responsibility of religious leaders to emphasize that peace and tolerance have to be promoted from the top down and nurtured from the bottom up. What religions can do, and, indeed, in instances of interfaith conflicts, must do, is point out emphatically to those who would make war that religion will not be a party to inhumane practices and does not condone killing or the persecution of any group because of its ethnic or religious background. Regardless of differences in culture, religion, or language, a civil society and a lasting peace can come only from the hearts of the people, aided and abetted by leaders of faith and conscience.

8

The United Religions Initiative at Work

Charles Gibbs

Two days into a United Religions Initiative East Africa conference in Nairobi, Kenya, in May 1998, participants began commenting: I am a Muslim and I was afraid to come here because I thought I would have to sit down with a Christian. Or, I am a Christian and I was afraid to come here because I thought I was going to have to sit down with a Muslim. Both Muslims and Christians continued: But I conquered my fear and came. And I'm glad that I did. Because I did have to sit down with a Christian/Muslim and I discovered that it wasn't so bad. Yes, we have differences, but we want the same kind of future and I believe we can work together.

F OR THE PAST FIVE YEARS the United Religions Initiative (URI) has engaged in an expanding global interfaith dialogue on how to create an organization dedicated to interfaith peacebuilding on a grassroots level around the world. The central articulation of the results of this inquiry is found in the URI's charter, signed in June 2000. The charter begins: "We, people of diverse religions, spiritual expressions and indigenous traditions throughout the world, hereby establish the

United Religions Initiative to promote enduring, daily interfaith cooperation, to end religiously motivated violence and to create cultures of peace, justice and healing for the Earth and all living beings." The URI is an experiment in a new form of interfaith dialogue and a new way of organizing. This experiment holds great promise for the creation of a global network of circles dedicated to enduring daily interfaith cooperation for peace, justice, and healing. In addition to being a proactive force for peace, this network will be a resource to help transform zones of interfaith conflict into zones of interfaith peace. The experiment is still young, but it has some insights to offer about interfaith dialogue and peacebuilding.

The seed that has grown into the URI was planted in the winter of 1993 when the Episcopal bishop of San Francisco, William Swing, was invited to host an interfaith service at Grace Cathedral in June 1995 as part of the commemoration of the fiftieth anniversary of the signing of the UN Charter in San Francisco. From this invitation was born the vision that has animated the URI since its inception: the creation of a global forum where the religions of the world would meet on a daily basis in mutual respect, prayerful dialogue, and cooperative action to make peace among religions so that they might become a compelling force for global good. This vision and the organizational design that goes with it have evolved tremendously since 1993 but at the center remain a commitment to interfaith cooperation for global good.

The effort to create a truly global URI took wing in June 1996 at the URI's first global summit. Up to that point this vision of a spiritual analogue to the United Nations had been held by a small interfaith group in San Francisco. Bishop Swing had led an opportunistic effort to share this vision with religious and interfaith leaders around the world, but there had been no systematic attempt to develop a globally shared vision. Imagining that effort was to be the focus of the URI's first global summit.

Central to the summit's success and the success of the URI's subsequent efforts was the coming together of the URI vision with the work of appreciative inquiry (AI), an innovative methodology for organizational development pioneered around the world by David Cooperrider and colleagues of the Weatherhead School of Management at Case Western University, Cleveland, Ohio, through the Social Innovations in Global Management (SIGMA) and Global Excellence in Management (GEM) programs.

In the URI context, AI has proved itself, again and again, to be a powerful tool for bringing together people from diverse backgrounds. Grounded in a belief that calling a group to focus on a problem creates a practice of deficit thinking and ties people to what has failed in the past, AI asks people to recall and share the best of their past experience.

> We have all been part of efforts where we have joined with others and brought dreams of a better world into being. For the moment I would like you to reflect on a "high point" in your life experience—a time when you were involved in something significant or meaningful. Reflect on a time when perhaps . . .
>
> ◆ your deepest energies were called upon;
> ◆ you gave your whole best self to something;
> ◆ you were listening, perhaps with a spiritual ear, to what the world was calling for from you and others;
> ◆ whole new paths or possibilities emerged;
> ◆ changes, small or large, were made that at first seemed impossible;
> ◆ visions of a better world were actually brought into being.
>
> Please share with me the story and how it unfolded. Without being too humble, please share what you contributed to this effort. Are there lessons that might be brought to this gathering?
>
> Each of our communities of faith has special gifts—traditions, beliefs, practices, values—to bring to the arena of interfaith cooperation and action. As you think about your community of faith, what are some of its most positive qualities or gifts that make it capable of working cooperatively with others of different faiths to create a better world for all people?
>
> ◆ Are there special texts or passages or quotes that stand out for you?
> ◆ A story or parable?
> ◆ Historical experiences?
> ◆ Capabilities, commitments, or values?
>
> Please share these with me.[1]

The personal experiences and the valuing of our diverse traditions such questions evoke, and the relationships that are created as the answers are shared in one-on-one interviews and then in small groups, provide a foundation of trust, mutual respect, and a recognition of common ground in the midst of diversity. They create a climate of careful listening and a spirit of cooperation and inquiry. Building on this foundation, participants cocreate a positive vision of a shared future powerful enough to motivate the cooperative action necessary to transform the past.

At the URI's first global summit, AI enabled a diverse group of fifty-five people—not only religious and spiritual leaders but also people from a wide array of vocations in business, the arts, education, healing, science, and so on—to forge a shared positive vision of the future and to outline a plan to begin to realize that future. In this case, the shared vision and planning focused on how to create a global inquiry around the possibility of a global URI.

In discovering appreciative inquiry, the URI found a process for creating an organization that reflected the values we felt the organization should embody. At the center of those values was a belief in the essential nature of interfaith cooperation that honors, indeed celebrates, diversity, and yet constantly strives to discover a common vision leading to shared action for a better world.

Out of that first summit came a plan to share the URI's animating vision globally in an attempt to elicit the visions and participation of people all over the world. This growing global appreciative inquiry, which unfolded over the next four years, came to include religious, spiritual, and indigenous leaders from a wide array of traditions, as well as secular leaders from the same array of traditions and a broad range of vocations. It has asked them to imagine the world they would like to live in: the world they would like to see children grow up in and adults grow old in. It has asked them how they could imagine their tradition and all religions, spiritual expressions, and indigenous traditions together contributing to making this vision a reality.

Through this global inquiry, a locally particular and globally consistent picture of a United Religions Initiative, which was far different from the founding vision, emerged. Though still dedicated to interfaith cooperation for global good, the vision was no longer of a centralized organization involving religious elites who would be mostly male providing direction for the rest of the world.

Instead, a vision evolved of an organization that was founded in the grass roots. It involved the equitable participation of women and men from a broad range of human vocations. In addition to the world's "great, historic religions," it welcomed spiritual expressions and indigenous traditions. It imagined an organizational structure that was globally connected through a shared purpose and principles but locally rooted and relevant in terms of decision making and action. Its foundational values included hospitality, the importance of being deeply rooted in our own traditions, the celebration of diversity, the inclusion of voices not often heard, and the belief expressed by Gandhi that we must be the change we wish to see in the world.

In the process of this global inquiry, the URI accomplished two things crucial to its future development. First, it created a charter that speaks with the voices of thousands of people from an astonishing array of religions, spiritual expressions, and indigenous traditions throughout the world. This charter, which frames an innovative organizational design and process of organizing, guides the work of a global network of Cooperation Circles that are free to organize in any manner, at any scale, and around any issue consistent with the charter. Second, the global inquiry created a growing community of people across the globe who are committed to making the high vision of interfaith cooperation expressed in the charter a lived reality.

Any peacebuilding effort must deal with a confluence of the past, the present, and the future. Often it is past oppression, injustice, and violence that ignite violence in the present and extend it indefinitely into the future. By its creation of a globally shared charter and a growing global community dedicated to making this charter a lived reality, the URI seeks to intervene in this cycle by calling people of diverse religions, spiritual expressions, and indigenous traditions to explore the past in a different way—to mine the past for the raw materials that will enable us to create a shared vision of a positive future and the commitment to work cooperatively to make that vision a reality.

As noted, the URI is still young and its experiment is just beginning to unfold. Still, there are some examples from our four-year global inquiry and the year since the charter signing that indicate the URI's potential.

First, let's return to the URI East Africa conference in May 1998 where Christians and Muslims discovered that they did not need to be afraid to sit down with each other and that they did not need to be afraid to sit down with Hindus or Sikhs or Baha'is or animists either. Many seeds were planted during that conference, which saw fifty-eight people come together from eight countries (Kenya, Uganda, Ethiopia, Tanzania, Rwanda, Burundi, Sudan, and Somalia). There were twenty women and thirty-eight men from fourteen religious-spiritual traditions (twenty-nine Christians: seventeen Protestants, six Roman Catholics, five Orthodox, and one Evangelical; seven Muslims; six Baha'is; four Brahma Kumaris; three Sikhs; two animists; two Theosophists; one Hindu; one Jew; three not designated); eight young people also attended.

A lack of resources to tend each seed carefully and the attrition that is natural in any organization meant that not all the seeds that were planted took root, sent up shoots, and bore fruit. But many did. On a trip to Africa in January 2001, I saw some of those fruits firsthand. In Kampala, Uganda, we had a daylong workshop with twelve Cooperation Circles (CCs) whose work includes interfaith dialogue, education, AIDS prevention, economic development, and conflict transformation. Among the plans to emerge that day was the development of conflict transformation workshops that would provide training of trainers for all twelve CCs so that they might be more effective forces for peace in their local communities.

The Cooperation Circle in Nairobi, Kenya, was active in the days following the bombing of the U.S. embassy in 1998. It staged an interfaith peace service and helped in a ceremony planting a peace pole dedicated to the victims of the bombing. The following message expresses something of the URI's global community:

January 27, 1999

To Our Dear Sisters and Brothers in Nairobi,

Greetings of love and peace in the name of the United Religions Initiative from your sisters and brothers of all faiths from all parts of the world.

We applaud you and stand with you as witnesses for peace and interreligious cooperation in the face of the tragedy that took human lives in Dar-es-Salaam and Nairobi this past August 7. We join you in honoring the victims of those explosions.

By standing together for peace, you send a message of hope to people all over the world who have grown weary of violence and hatred. To those who have tired of the path of distrust, hatred, and destruction, you send the compelling message that we can dare to choose the path of mutual respect, peace, and cooperative action for the good of all.

May your gathering be a source of inspiration and blessing to all who participate, and to a war weary world seeking a more hopeful day. May all people live in peace. May peace prevail on earth.

In Addis Ababa, Ethiopia, the local Cooperation Circle inaugurated the first URI subregional office outside San Francisco. The CC members were a consistent force for interfaith peacebuilding during the war between Ethiopia and Eritrea. A plaque with the following text hung on the wall of the office:

"On the Occasion of the first National Conference on
Building a Culture of Peace—Character, Family
and Public Service"
The United Nations Association of Ethiopia, Family Federation
for World Peace and United Nations Volunteers Program
Hereby awarded this
Certificate of Merit
to
United Religions Initiative

In recognition of its outstanding Contribution in Pioneering in
Ethiopia for the first time interfaith dialogue among diverse
religious groups to build a Culture of Peace and create harmony.
This Certificate of Merit is given on this 22nd, December 2000.

These are small fruits, growing from tiny seeds of hope planted in the ground of shared visions of a future where hatred is transformed by the healing power of sacrificial love, where violence is transformed into peace, where children are not recruited into distrust, enmity, and violence but into mutual respect, cooperation, and peace. It will take many years to see if this garden will grow into the fullness of its potential. But even at this early stage its potential is great and the fruit that is growing is changing local communities and through them the world.

Another example of the URI's developing work comes from the Americas. While there seems to be no major interfaith conflict in the Americas, an interfaith toxic waste pollutes the waters of life from northernmost Alaska to Tierra del Fuego. Its roots extend back more than five hundred years, sunk in the soil of the Christian conquest and destruction of native culture and spiritual practice. This decidedly interfaith toxicity exacts each day a hidden toll. This toll is difficult to measure, like the effects of any toxic waste, and yet there can be no true peace and wholeness in the Americas as long as this toxicity endures.

1562

> Fray Diego de Landa throws into the flames, one after the other, the books of the Mayas.
>
> The inquisitor curses Satan, and the fire crackles and devours. Around the incinerator, heretics howl with their heads down. Hung by the feet, flayed with whips, Indians are doused with boiling wax as the fire flares up and the books snap, as if complaining.
>
> Tonight, eight centuries of Mayan literature turn to ashes. On these long sheets of bark paper, signs and images spoke: They told of work done and days spent, of the dreams and the wars of a people born before Christ. With hog-bristle brushes, the knowers of things had painted these illuminated, illuminating books so that the grandchildren's grandchildren should not be blind, should know how to see themselves and see the history of their folk, so they should know the movements of the stars, the frequency of eclipses and the prophecies of the gods and so they could call for rains and good corn harvests.
>
> In the center, the inquisitor burns the books. Around the huge bonfire, he chastises the readers.[2]

We have a choice to ignore this toxicity and its causes, and to continue to suffer its destructive consequences, or to confront it and work cooperatively in the hopes that one day these waters may once again run clear and be a source of life for all. The need for healing is great, but the path to that healing leads through the very communities that first sought to destroy the First Peoples and now seek to ignore them. Our successful work in this endeavor will be a harbinger of much broader success in interfaith peacebuilding efforts designed to deal with a toxic past in ways that create the conditions for peace long before violent conflict erupts.

As noted, the URI did not begin with the vision that it would be a force for peace, justice, and healing between and among indigenous peoples and their oppressors. Yet, as our global inquiry unfolded, it became increasingly clear that it should involve people from all parts of the human family. Because of the history and present practice of oppression and persecution of native peoples around the world, and because it seemed especially important in this time of environmental crisis that their spiritual wisdom about Earth be part of the conversation, the URI made an effort to include indigenous peoples in framing the vision of what this new organization could be and what it should do. In choosing consciously to seek out indigenous people to participate in our work, we created and sought out contexts in which to hear their stories.

> URI Summit, Buenos Aires, 1997—Two different indigenous women, Haydee Milimay, a Ranquel whose name means "Golden Condor," and Rosalia Guittierez, of the Kolla people, spoke with cautious hope that they would be able to share something about their traditions because they believed that there was a great deal of value in their traditions but that they weren't respected. Rosalia told me that she could barely speak any of her native language because her grandparents had had their tongues cut out so they wouldn't be able to teach their language to their children!

> Prayer Vigil for the Earth, Washington, D.C., 2000—So many moving stories of the pain and suffering of indigenous peoples stripped of their culture, punished for trying to hold on to their culture, and until 1976 having it illegal, in this land that guarantees freedom of religion, to pray in a native way. But also soaring spirits of determination and transformation as the peoples reclaim their cultures and spiritual practices, breathe new life into them and use them, as fuel and inspiration to struggle for a new day. A new day for the sacred Mother Earth. A new day founded in prayer.

> Clyde Bellecourt, an Ojibway man, spoke movingly of learning from his mother, after he nearly died from a gunshot wound at Wounded Knee, of the hardships she endured when she was forcibly removed from her home and placed in a boarding school where she was forced to clean floors on her knees with a toothbrush if she was caught speaking her language or praying in a native way; forced, finally, to do this wearing kneepads with marbles in them; then hiding this from her children so they wouldn't grow up with bitterness.[3]

With this hearing came a growing awareness of the issues native peoples up and down the Americas deal with daily and of the implied commitment to do something to ameliorate those conditions. We came to see, in a wisdom that exists in all spiritual traditions and that was articulated by Martin Luther King Jr., "that their destiny is tied up with our destiny. . . . We cannot walk alone."[4]

In fact, we are no longer walking alone. In October 2000, the URI sponsored a conference in Quito, Ecuador, attended by sixty indigenous people from ten pueblos: Nahual (Nicaragua); Miskito (Nicaragua); Kuna (Panama); Mapuche (Chile); Maya (Guatemala and Mexico); Shuar (Ecuador); Kolla (Argentina); Quichua (Ecuador); Aymara (Bolivia); and Inca (Peru). For three days they shared their "cosmovisiones," making it clear that there is no distinction between religion and culture, between the sacred and the secular in these indigenous views of the cosmos. They also made it clear what a devastating toll the European conquest had taken on their traditions. A Nahual man from Nicaragua gave the following explanation:

> Colonization, primarily by other religions, has been a damaging factor for the Nahual. We have lost our land, lost our language. We have a fractured culture that we are struggling to reclaim. We honor the Earth, and are conscious about wise resource use. But so much has been lost—culture, history, education. Our sad reality is that we have lost our cosmovision and our practice of spirituality. We are seeking out Nahuals from other countries and other sisters and brothers—the Mayans, for instance—to try to recreate our cosmovision. Religion is a force that divides us. For instance, my mother is Roman Catholic and my brother is Protestant and they have a very hard time being together because of their religious differences.

By the end of these three days, there was a strong sense of solidarity among these diverse peoples. They delighted in the common ground they had discovered among themselves and they valued their diversity and uniqueness. They left with a strong commitment to support each other in their efforts to reclaim their sacred traditions and to explore dialogue with the colonizing religions (primarily different branches of Christianity), even recognizing that some who attended this conference were fed by both their indigenous cosmovision and

Christianity. The path to healing and wholeness is not fully clear, but this group took a courageous and historic step down that path.

Another step down that path came in North America. At the first URI North America Regional Summit in Salt Lake City, Utah, in May 2001, representatives of the First Peoples of Turtle Island (North America) chose to form a Cooperation Circle that will ensure that their voices will be an important part of the ongoing work of the URI. This decision presents the whole of the URI with a great gift and an even greater challenge, which is to listen deeply to what these voices have to say and to join our voices with their voices, our hearts with their hearts, and our hands with their hands in working to clean up the interfaith toxic waste that threatens our community—the Earth community.

So we take small steps in a grand experiment to live in a new model of interfaith dialogue and peacebuilding grounded in appreciation and inquiry. Many seeds are sown. Some are beginning to bear modest fruit. The potential for a bountiful harvest is great, but so is the need that these seeds, seedlings, and young plants be nurtured. The global community of the URI is committed to this nurturing.

The following is a final image that represents the positive future the URI seeks to build:

In May 1999, the URI cosponsored an interfaith conference in Brazil with Pallas Athena, a center for the study of religion and culture; the World Business Academy; and ISER, a Rio de Janeiro–based organization that specializes in research to support practical work to address social problems in Brazil. One hundred twenty-five people from thirty-five different religious, spiritual, and indigenous traditions attended. Though there have been many interfaith efforts in Brazil for decades, this was the first time representatives from most of them, as well as individuals from diverse traditions engaged in a wide variety of vocations, had met together.

The gathering provided an essential opportunity to make known and to celebrate existing interfaith work and to begin to forge strategic alliances for future work. Also, those present engaged with the URI vision and explored how connecting existing Brazilian interfaith work to this global initiative might be mutually beneficial. An image of the future we wish to create materialized on the extraordinary evening of the second day.

Around a bonfire, under a full moon, on a mountain in the Brazilian rain forest, representatives from four indigenous nations shared a ritual of sacred dance and chant. Each nation did its unique dance, and then all four shared a common dance. We learned later that this was a great breakthrough for these peoples. They had never danced together before. The previous night, as they talked about leading the whole group in shared sacred ritual, they reached the conclusion that if they were to be a force for healing and peace for the whole group they must first make peace among themselves. The manifestation of that peace was their shared dance.

At the end of the shared dance, the rest of the group was invited to dance. We joined hands and danced ourselves into exhaustion. At one point, I looked around the circle and saw indigenous people in their native dress, a Zen Buddhist monk in her robes, a Tibetan Buddhist monk in his robes, two Dominican monks in their robes, and a Hindu swami in his robes. I saw all sizes, shapes, ages, and colors of men and women in regular clothes and in ritual clothes, hands joined, dancing together as one community, extraordinarily diverse and yet united. In that moment, it felt as though we were living our visions of a better world. We were what we seek to become.

That is our goal. That is our commitment.

NOTES

1. From the notebook prepared for participants at URI's first global summit.

2. Eduardo Galeano, *Memory of Fire: I. Genesis,* trans. Cedric Belfrage (New York: W. W. Norton, 1985), 137.

3. These passages are taken from the author's travel journals.

4. Martin Luther King Jr., "I Have A Dream," in *A Testament of Hope* (San Francisco: Harper and Row, 1968), 218.

Conclusion

David R. Smock

ELIGION IS CITED AS A CAUSE OF INTERNATIONAL CONFLICTS more frequently than the facts would warrant. When religion is a factor it is usually one of several interrelated causal factors such as ethnicity, economic disparities, and regional differences. One of the contributors to this volume, Arthur Schneier, goes so far as to assert that religion is never the cause of conflict, although it is often identified as an excuse for other causes. Other authors see religion as one of several causal components. One author, Joseph Leichty, cites religion as being a central element, although not the only one, in the conflict in Northern Ireland. Leichty devotes his chapter to an exposition of a methodology, which he terms mitigation, that can be used to ameliorate religious conflict in Northern Ireland and elsewhere when theological differences feed intergroup tensions. Mitigation permits adherents to a faith to still cling to their most basic convictions even when those beliefs are diametrically opposed to the beliefs of those in the other community. Mitigation permits sharp differences in religious belief while minimizing the divisive social consequences of embracing those positions.

Interfaith dialogue can be of great value in ameliorating conflict and advancing reconciliation even when religion is not the central cause of a conflict. If the opposing groups are differentiated by religious identity, then interfaith dialogue can be productively employed. Organizing dialogue across religious boundaries enables people of faith to live out what most faith traditions consider as a sacred duty to be peacemakers.

Interfaith dialogue carries with it the benefits of secular dialogue but also the potential for deeper and more meaningful engagement because of the possibility for spiritual encounter. This in turn may enhance the participants' commitment to peace work and social change. The use of rituals and religious symbols is a special feature of interfaith dialogue, distinguishing it from interethnic dialogue. The use of scripture and sacred texts in dialogue settings also differentiates interfaith inter-action, allowing the dialogue to reach a deeper level of authenticity.

The depth of passion that accompanies interfaith dialogue also carries with it liabilities. Sharing at the deep level of religious convic-tion can generate resistance and defensiveness. Interreligious conversa-tion can provoke intolerance of the religious narratives of others. Ronald Young notes that interreligious discussion of the Middle East conflict forces Christians, Jews, and Muslims to confront some of their deepest fears and most persistent prejudices about one another. To engage in interfaith dialogue also runs the risk of inflaming stereotypes and prejudices against one's own group.

Interfaith dialogue can be directed to several levels of religious leadership. Organizations such as the Appeal of Conscience Foun-dation work with the top echelons of religious hierarchies. The prin-cipal purpose of the foundation's projects is to support the peace-making efforts of such secular bodies as the United Nations. This foundation and the World Conference on Religion and Peace have also been effective in facilitating the organization of interreligious councils formed of high-level representatives from the faith communities. In his work in the Balkans, David Steele has concluded that it is most pro-ductive to work at the middle ranges of religious leadership, engaging both clergy and lay leaders. He has found that these participants then influence others in their religious communities. The original intention of the United Religions Initiative (URI) was to engage religious elites, but the URI concluded that it could have a greater impact by working at the community level. The URI seeks to facilitate deep spiritual shar-ing among persons of different faiths at the grass roots and then help its Cooperation Circles to engage in joint activities. Each of these approaches complements the others and addresses an important part of the overall interfaith project.

Interfaith dialogue can take different forms and seek different ends. For instance, dialogue can have as its principal purpose the preparation of a joint declaration or it can seek to improve relationships among participants in the dialogue. Despite this diversity, we can nevertheless identify principles that help determine the quality of the outcome of the dialogue process.

◆ The dialogue needs to have a clear purpose.

◆ It is crucial to select the right participants—those who are sincerely committed to peace and who will be good listeners. Participants need to be ready and able to hear the stories and convictions of those on the other side. Participants also need to be well grounded in their own faith and to be positioned to influence the thinking of members of their wider faith community after the dialogue ends.

◆ Smaller groups generally lend themselves to more irenic dialogue than do larger groups.

◆ It may be valuable to start by having each faith group meet separately to explore the participants' positions on controversial issues and to establish group identity. This also permits clarification of what each faith tradition has to say on critical issues to be discussed with the other community.

◆ It is important to address imbalances in power among the groups participating. This is to ensure that symmetric arrangements are made in the process and the design of the dialogue. The selection of the language or languages to be used is critical in this equation.

◆ The dialogue needs to explore both the similarities among the participating faiths and the core differences that divide them.

◆ It is valuable to spend time on healing and acknowledging collective and individual injuries—walking through history. Some of the most effective interfaith dialogue processes focus on storytelling—giving participants an opportunity to share their suffering and to be assured that their hurts are being taken seriously by those on the other side. Dialogue should give sensitive and compassionate attention to the emotions of grief, fear, and anger. Storytelling can also enable participants to confront their fear of the future.

◆ Dialogue has the potential for helping participants deal with their sense of victimization, a feeling usually shared by participants on both sides.

◆ A central goal should be to address misperceptions and to break down stereotypes that each group holds regarding the other.

◆ The dialogue process should aim at building relationships between participating individuals and between communities, both within the dialogue setting and over the longer term. Intergroup reconciliation should be an overarching goal.

◆ Apology and forgiveness can be powerful components of interfaith dialogue. Effective dialogue requires openness to sharing the suffering of the other side and to recognizing the sins and shortcomings of one's own side.

◆ The process should seek to achieve greater consensus about the truth relating to divisive issues.

◆ The long-term goal of dialogue must go beyond building relationships to address the justice issues that may have provoked the conflict and the structural issues that have generated the grievances. Dialogue that contributes to peace needs to confront the political issues lying behind violent conflict.

◆ One purpose of interfaith dialogue may be to teach participants conflict resolution skills.

◆ Another goal may be to prepare a joint public declaration relating to peace and reconciliation. But the preparation of such a declaration may inhibit participants from sharing some of their deepest grievances.

◆ Successful dialogue can help the opposing sides to move away from a cycle of revenge.

◆ Dialogue can often identify peacebuilding resources within participants' faith traditions.

◆ Religious leaders and clergy should not be the only participants in dialogue. Laypersons can also benefit from and
contribute to the process.

◆ One-time dialogue sessions are often of only limited value.
A series of sessions is desirable, as are various kinds of
follow-up to the series of sessions.

◆ A severe limitation of interfaith dialogue is that many faith
groups are not willing to participate, either because of the
dictates of their faith convictions or because of the level of
animosity they bear toward the other religious group.
Unfortunately, it is these groups that are often the main pro-
tagonists in the conflict.

◆ Interfaith dialogue rarely ends wars, but it can contribute to
the development of a peaceful solution and it can aid the
process of reconciliation in postconflict periods.

When interfaith dialogue is confined to talk and conversation,
Marc Gopin asserts, little is accomplished. Dialogue favors those with
verbal skills and those who are more aggressive; it disadvantages those
individuals or groups who are less verbally gifted. Other authors join
Gopin in concluding that interfaith interaction that goes beyond talk
and entails joint activities can be much more powerful. The shared
study of sacred texts is one such activity and can be particularly valuable
for religions like Islam, Judaism, and Christianity that share reverence
for their basic texts. Such study can enhance mutual understanding and
may also identify shared values, for instance, the belief in the sacredness
of Jerusalem that is common to the three Abrahamic faiths. Even more
powerful are symbolic acts of apology undertaken on a reciprocal basis,
such as Jews in the Middle East helping to rebuild damaged mosques
and Muslim cemeteries, and Muslims mourning Jews killed in political
violence. Words communicated in dialogue can be powerfully supple-
mented by deeds and symbols aimed at transforming relationships.

Contributors

Mohammed Abu-Nimer is a professor at American University in Washington, D.C., where he specializes in peace and conflict resolution studies. He has conducted research on conflict resolution among Palestinians and Jews in Israel, on the application of conflict resolution models in non-Western contexts, and on Islam and peacebuilding. He has conducted conflict resolution training workshops in Israel, Palestine, Egypt, Sri Lanka, Northern Ireland, the Philippines, and the United States. His most recent book is *Reconciliation, Justice, Coexistence: Theory and Practice* (Lanham, Md.: Lexington Books, 2001).

Jaco Cilliers has worked on conflict resolution in multireligious communities in several parts of the world. He is currently the justice and peacebuilding senior advisor for Catholic Relief Services. He holds a Ph.D. from the Institute for Conflict Analysis and Resolution at George Mason University, Fairfax, Virginia.

The Rev. Canon Charles Gibbs serves as the executive director of the United Religions Initiative, an interfaith organization active on every continent with its global office in San Francisco, California, and which is dedicated to creating cultures of peace, justice, and healing. He is an Episcopalian priest.

Marc Gopin is visiting associate professor of international diplomacy at the Fletcher School for Law and Diplomacy, senior researcher at its Institute for Human Security, and a visiting scholar at Harvard University's Program on Negotiation. He is author of *Between Eden and Armageddon: The Future of World Religions, Violence, and Peacemaking* (New York and London: Oxford University Press, 2000) and *Holy War, Holy Peace: How Religion Can Bring Peace to the Middle East* (New York: Oxford University Press, 2002).

Joseph Liechty, a Mennonite Board of Missions worker, is lecturer in reconciliation studies for the Irish School of Ecumenics at Trinity College Dublin. He is author with Cecelia Clegg of *Moving Beyond Sectarianism: Religion, Conflict, and Reconciliation in Northern Ireland* (Blackrock, County Dublin: Columba Press, 2001).

Rabbi Arthur Schneier is founder and president of the Appeal of Conscience Foundation, launched in 1965, and has been spiritual leader of New York's Park East Synagogue since 1962. He has served as U.S. alternate representative to the UN General Assembly, as chairman of the Commission for the Preservation of America's Heritage Abroad, and as a member of the first religious delegation to China to promote religious tolerance. A Holocaust survivor, he received the 2001 Presidential Citizens Medal for his lifetime dedication to overcoming the forces of hatred and intolerance. He has worked to encourage interfaith dialogue in many countries and convened four religious summits on peace and tolerance in the former Yugoslavia. In 2001 he initiated the Resolution for the Protection of Religious Sites adopted by the UN General Assembly.

David Smock is director of the Religion and Peacemaking Initiative at the United States Institute of Peace. He was previously director of the Grants program and coordinator of Africa activities at the Institute. Earlier he was posted to several parts of Africa and the Middle East by the Ford Foundation. He is the author and editor of several books on religion and on Africa. He is an ordained minister of the United Church of Christ.

David Steele is director of a project on religion and conflict resolution in the former Yugoslavia at the Center for Strategic and International Studies. In addition to facilitating interfaith dialogue and training events, he works with political leaders in the former Yugoslavia to resolve conflicts. He is an ordained minister of the United Church of Christ and holds a Ph.D. in Christian ethics and practical theology from the University of Edinburgh.

Ronald Young is executive director of the U.S. Interreligious Committee for Peace in the Middle East, a national organization founded in 1987 with 2,500 American Jews, Christians, and Muslims as members. He worked with the Quakers in the Middle East from 1982 to 1985 and is author of *Missed Opportunities for Peace: U.S. Middle East Policy, 1981–1986* (Philadelphia: American Friends Service Committee, 1987).

Index

Abrahamic faiths
  antimodernist fundamentalism
    in, 41
  in Arab-Israeli conflict, 39–40
  claim of each to be exclusive
    way to salvation, 93–94
  forgiveness and compassion in,
    54
  importance of relations with
    neighbor and God in,
    75–76
  importance of sacred places in,
    3, 70, 112–113, 131
  importance of self-examina-
    tion in, 77
  sense of dependence on God
    in, 75
  value of all human beings
    affirmed in, 77
Abu-Nimer, Mohammed, 10,
  15–29
ACF. See Appeal of Conscience
  Foundation (ACF)
advocate's role, in peacebuilding,
  73
aggression, 38–39, 77, 80
  humanization of aggressor,
    80
Ajzenkol, Marijana, 86, 87
Albanians, in Kosovo, 110
Americas, interfaith toxic waste
  in, 122–126
anti-Catholicism, 97–99
  mitigation of, 98, 99
  in Northern Ireland, 97–99
anti-Semitism, Christian responsibility for, 70

apartheid, religious pursuit of
  justice during, 51–52
apology, forgiveness and, 83, 131
Appeal of Conscience
  Foundation (ACF), 10, 76,
    105–106, 128
  approaches to interfaith dia-
    logue, 106–107
  in Bosnia, 107–111
  Bosphorus Conference, 109
  Inter-Religious Council of
    Bosnia-Herzegovina, 110
  in Kosovo, 110–111
  operations in conflict situa-
    tions, 107–110
  use of electronic media, 113
Appleby, R. Scott, 7
appreciative inquiry (AI),
  116–118
Arab Americans, Middle East
  issues and, 67–68
Arab-Israeli conflict. See Middle
  East conflict
Arafat, Yasir, 65
Argentina, indigenous peoples
  in, 124
Assefa, Hiskiaz, 50
Aymara people, 124

balance of power. See power
Bartholomew I, Patriarch, 109
Bašalić, Jagoda, 79
Belfast Agreement, Protestant
  opposition to, 90
Bellecourt, Clyde, 123
betrayal, sense of, forgiveness
  and, 83

Bible
  book of Jeremiah, 81–82
  Jesus' teachings and mitiga-
    tion, 99–100
  Old Testament, 81–82
Bolivia, indigenous peoples in,
  124
Bosnia-Herzegovina
  Appeal of Conscience work in,
    107–111
  Center for Religious Dialogue,
    86
  declaration to end killing in,
    108–109
  Inter-religious Center in, 86,
    87
  Inter-Religious Council, 110
  peacebuilding in, 74, 79,
    80–81, 82, 85, 87–88
  reconciliation initiative in, 53
Bosnian Serb Republic, peace-
  building in, 74, 79, 88
Bosphorus Conference (Istanbul,
  1994), 109
both/and reasoning, employed in
  conflict analysis, 89–90
Buddhism
  Four Noble Truths, 51
  justice within, 51

Camp David treaty (1979), 64
Catholic Church
  anti-Catholicism, 97–99
  attitude toward Jews and
    Judaism, 42–43
  Congregation for the Doctrine
    of the Faith, 96
  doctrine of inerrancy, 43
  Dominus Iesus, 96
  evaluation of papal behavior,
    43
  evaluation of Protestantism,
    95–97

during Holocaust, 43
  One Bread, One Body, 95–97
Catholics, 19
  in Bosnia-Herzegovina,
    80–81, 85, 108–109
  in Kosovo, 110–111
  in Northern Ireland, 3, 89–101
  See also Catholic Church
Center for Religious Dialogue
  (CRD), 86, 88
Center for Strategic and
  International Studies
  (CSIS), 74, 77, 88
Center for the Study of Conflict,
  90
Chile, indigenous peoples in, 124
Chosen People, 23
Christianity
  claim of exclusive salvation
    through, 93–94
  concept of justice in, 51
  forgiveness and healing in, 27,
    100
  Islam and, 3–4, 69
  Judaism and, 69
  mitigation resources in,
    99–100
  nonnegotiability of religious
    ideas in, 92
  responsibility for anti-
    Semitism and Holocaust, 70
  study in, 41
Christians
  beliefs and practices of, 19, 20,
    23
  dialogue on Middle East with
    Muslims and Jews, 10, 23
  Filipino, 19
  U.S., Middle East issues and,
    66–70
  See also Christianity; *specific
    denominations*
Church of Ireland, doctrinal

statements by, 97
Cilliers, Jaco, 10, 47–58
Clegg, Cecelia, 91
collaborative task, inclusion of in
    interfaith dialogue, 23–24
colonization, 124
communion. *See* Eucharist
Community of Sant'Egidio, 4
compromise
    as mitigation skill, 91–92
    on religious ideas, 92–94
Conference of European
    Churches, 76
conflict
    analysis of, 35, 54, 89–90
    compromise as skill in miti-
        gating, 91–92
    relatedness of family, intercul-
        tural, and international, 34
    transformation of through
        spirituality, 17
conflict resolution, 130
    fundamental crux of, 36
    indigenous method of, 39
    training in, 8, 17, 34
    use of media in, 113
Conflict Resolution Conference
    (Vienna, 1995), 109–110,
    111
conflict transformation
    interfaith dialogue as part of,
        45
    peacebuilding and, 56–57
    through acknowledging
        wrongdoing, 25
    See also transformation
Congregation for the Doctrine of
    the Faith, 96
cooperation, interfaith, in
    Middle East, 64–72
Cooperation Circles, 119,
    120–121, 125
Cooperrider, David, 116–117

"Coping with Calamity" seminar,
    79
Coser, Lewis, 48
CRD. *See* Center for Religious
    Dialogue (CRD)
Croatia
    peacebuilding in, 78, 84
    treatment of minorities in,
        84–85
Crusades, 17–18, 68
CSIS. *See* Center for Strategic
    and International Studies
    (CSIS)
cues, nonverbal, 36
Curle, Adam, 58

deeds
    conflict resolution and, 36
    leading to peace and justice, 45
    of reconciliation, 8, 10, 33–34,
        37–38, 131
deficit thinking, 117
Derviŝalija, Hodžić, 80
destruction of holy sites,
    112–113
destructive consequences, mitiga-
    tion of, 95
dialogue
    cross-community, 8
    debate versus, 6
    deeds of reconciliation versus
        words, 8, 10, 34, 35, 37–38,
        131
    development of new sensitivity
        to language, 15
    during conflict, 10
    elasticity of method for, 35–36
    inherent exclusion in, 44
    interethnic, 20
    reconciliation and, 35–36, 37
    social action and, 15–16
    as stimulus for improving com-
        munity, 15

dialogue *(cont.)*
   turning point in process, 15
   use of term as equivalent of
    peacemaking and conflict res-
    olution, 34
   words in context of, 34–35
   See also interfaith dialogue
differences, examination of in
   interfaith dialogue, 22–23
diversity, importance of in interfaith organizations, 119
domination, as issue in conflicts,
   91
Dominus Iesus, 96
Dunn, Seamus, 90–91

Eck, Diane, 6–7
ECONI. *See* Evangelical
   Contribution on Northern
   Ireland (ECONI)
Ecuador, indigenous peoples in, 124
ecumenical organizations, importance of in resolving religious
   conflicts, 112
Ecumenical Patriarchate, 109
educator's role, in peacebuilding,
   73, 74
Egypt
   Camp David treaty, 64
   interfaith leadership trips to, 65
   violence between Muslims and
    Christians in, 24
electronic media, use of to spread
   cooperation message, 113
elite leadership model, 7
emotional communication, in
   reconciliation, 35
empowerment, as result of interfaith dialogue, 28–29
enemies, loving in biblical teaching, 99–100
engagement
   deleterious processes of, 37

   missing cues of, 36
envy, 34
Eritrea, war with Ethiopia, 121
Ethiopia
   Cooperation Circle in, 121
   war with Eritrea, 121
ethnic cleansing, 80
   in Kosovo, 110
Eucharist
   Catholic practice of, 95–97
   shared, 96–97
Evangelical Contribution on
   Northern Ireland (ECONI),
   90
evangelicals, attitude of toward
   Catholic Church, 97

faith-based nongovernmental
   organizations, 9
family conflicts, representative of
   intercultural and international
   conflicts, 34–35
feelings, articulating with words,
   34
First Peoples, 122, 123, 125
Fojnica (Bosnia), problem-solving
   seminar in, 74, 85
follow-up issues, during peacebuilding, 85–86
forgiveness
   as form of love, 100
   in interfaith dialogue, 54–55,
    82–83
   justice and, 83–84
   revenge and, 82–83
   rituals of, 25
Four Noble Truths, in Buddhism,
   51
Friedman, Thomas, 4
fundamentalism, in Abrahamic
   faiths, 41

Gandhi, Mohandas, 119

Gaza
  interfaith leadership trips to, 65
  Israeli occupation of, 68
  U.S. Jews' beliefs about, 66
  See also Middle East conflict;
    Palestine
Gibbs, Charles, 10–11, 115–126
Global Excellence in Management
  (GEM) program, 117
globalization, versus tribalization,
  107
God, in Abrahamic faiths, 75
Good Friday Agreement. *See*
  Belfast Agreement
Gopin, Marc, 10, 33–45, 131
grieving of losses, 78–79
group psychology, as issue in large-
  group dialogues, 38–39
group size, importance of, 130
Gruchy, John de, 52
Guatemala, indigenous peoples in,
  124
Guittierez, Rosalia, 123

Halevi, Yossi Klein, 7
Hamas, 70
Haring, Bernard, 53
Hartman, Rabbi David, 4
healing, as aspect of interfaith dia-
  logue, 25
Hinduism, search for true mean-
  ing of, 55
Holocaust
  Catholic Church's behavior dur-
    ing, 43
  Christian responsibility for, 70
  Jewish experience of, 66
holy sites
  Christian interest in, 70
  conflicts over, 3
  importance of safety and preser-
    vation of, 40–41, 112–113,
    131

Holy Trinity, 23
Hrisistom, Bishop, 74, 88
human needs
  distinguished from positions on
    issues, 80
  identification of in interfaith
    dialogue, 79–81
humanism, as part of second language, 22–23
humanization, of aggressor, 80
humiliation, 34

Inca people, 124
inerrancy, doctrine of, 43
"infrastructure for peace," 57
injustice, recognition of, 54,
  129–130
Inquisition, 67–68
institution building, indigenous,
  88
interaction, flexibility in process of,
  24–25
interfaith cooperation, in Middle
  East, 64–72
interfaith council, importance of
  for interreligious cooperation,
  113
interfaith dialogue, 127–129
  as act as well as verbal commu-
    nication, 44
  avoidance of Middle East
    issues, 65
  as basis for creation of one
    world, 6–7
  clear purpose for, 129
  cognitive dimension of, 6
  concept of, 6, 47
  constructive approaches to,
    57–58
  controversial subjects in, 40
  distinguished from secular or
    interethnic encounters, 17
  empowerment and, 28–29

interfaith dialogue *(cont.)*
  foundations of, 50
    conflict transformation and
      peacebuilding, 56–57
    forgiveness, 54–55, 82–83, 130
    justice, 50–52, 130
    reconciliation, 52–54
    truth, 55–56, 130
  grassroots efforts, 8, 115–126
  group size in, 129
  highlighting theological and
    scriptural similarities, 8
  identification of basic human
    needs in, 79–81
  inclusion of the voiceless in, 44
  involvement of governments in,
    107
  measurable goals in, 45
  neutral third party used in,
    106–107
  organization of during conflict,
    8
  the "other" in, 49–50
  patterns of progression in,
    42–43
  peacebuilding and, 6, 8–9, 9–10,
    74–75
  peacemaking and, 38
  in postconflict period, 8
  power in, 21–22, 23, 24, 43, 129
  practical dimension of, 6, 131
  principles of, 21
    acknowledging and healing
      injuries, 8, 25, 81–82,
      129–130
    collaborative task inclusion,
      23–24
    examining similarities and
      differences, 22–23, 129
    flexibility of interaction
      process, 24–25
    selection of appropriate par-
      ticipants, 22, 129

  symmetric arrangements, 21
  unireligious preparation and
    forums, 25–26, 48–50, 129
  process of, 26–27
    first phase (excitement, ideal-
      ization), 27
    second phase (learning about
      differences and similari-
      ties), 22–23, 27–28, 129
    third phase (exploration of
      beliefs and values), 28
    fourth phase (empowerment
      and action), 28–29
  rituals in, 18–21
  spirituality in, 6, 16–18
  storytelling in, 10, 77–79
  as subset of wide range of trans-
    formational processes, 45
  targeted, 7–8
  terrorism as motivator for, 5
  time sensitivity of, 45
  as tool for peacebuilding, 8–9
  uniqueness of, 17
  unireligious preparation and
    forums, 25–26, 48–50, 129
  use of to move from good
    thoughts to good deeds, 45
  See also dialogue; interfaith
    cooperation
intermediary's role, in peacebuilding, 73
interreligious bodies, institutional-
  ization of, 13
Inter-religious Center (IRC), 86,
  87
Inter-Religious Council of Bosnia-
  Herzegovina, 110
Interreligious Council of Sierra
  Leone, 7
IRC. *See* Inter-religious Center
  (IRC)
Irish School of Ecumenics, 91
ISER, 125

Islam
Christianity and, 3–4
claim of exclusive salvation
through, 93–94
derivation of term, 27
idea of study in, 41
Judaism and, 3–4
justice and peace interconnected
in, 51
radical rhetoric of, 4
religious dialogue on, 4–5
role of in September 11 terrorist
attacks, 3–4
text-centered reverence in, 39
Western confrontation with,
39–40
isolation, forgiveness and, 83
Israel
Camp David treaty, 64
creation of, 66–67
holy sites in, 3
interfaith dialogue in, 39
interfaith leadership trips to, 65
Jews in, 23, 25
efforts with Palestinians
toward peace, 71
refusal to recognize
Palestinian right to self-
determination, 64
as victims and victimizers, 66
occupation of Gaza and West
Bank, 68
peace treaty with Jordan, 64
recognition of state of by Arabs
and Palestinians, 64
reliance of on world goodwill
and support, 67
security issues, 64
wars involving, 68
See also Middle East conflict
Israel Interfaith Association, 39
Israeli-PLO Declaration of
Principles (1993), 64

Jeremiah, 81–82
Jerusalem, importance of in Arab-
Israeli conflict, 40–41
Jesus, teachings of and mitigation,
99–100
Jews
ancient roots of, 27
dialogue on Middle East with
Christians and Muslims, 10,
21, 23–24
feelings during third phase of
dialogue, 28
Israeli, as victims and victimizers, 66
nationalism among, 69
seen as religious group, 69
self-perception as victims, 66
in U.S., 26
Middle East issues of, 66–67
reluctance to criticize Israel,
66
See also Israel, Jews in; Judaism
jihad, 23
Jordan, peace treaty with Israel
(1994), 64
Judaism
attitude of Catholic Church
toward, 42–43
claim of exclusive salvation
through, 93–94
Islam and, 3–4
lament motif in, 78–79,
81–82
Scriptures of, 81
text-centered reverence in,
39
Torah study in, 41–42
uncompromising faithfulness
in, 92
justice
absolute, 23
addressing through faith-based
approach, 51–52

justice *(cont.)*
  biblical understanding of, 90
  forgiveness and, 83–84
  as foundation of interfaith dia-
    logue, 50–52
  as issue in Northern Ireland, 90
  issues of underlying conflict, 10
  relationship to peace, 36

Kairos Document, 51–52
Karlovic, Bozidar, 78
Kenya
  bombing of U.S. embassy,
    120–121
  Cooperation Circle in, 120–121
King, Martin Luther, Jr., 124
Kolla people, 123, 124
Kosovo
  Albanians in, 110
  Appeal of Conscience
    Foundation work in,
    110–111
  Catholic bishop of, 111
  ethnic cleansing in, 110
  NATO bombing of, 79, 88, 111
  Orthodox bishop of, 111, 112
  peacebuilding in, 83
"Kosovo Peace and Tolerance,"
  111
Kristallnacht, 112
Kuna people, 124
Küng, Hans, 3, 48

Laden, Osama bin, 5
lament motif, in Judaism, 78–79,
  81–82
land, sacredness of, 40
Landa, Fray Diego de, 122
language
  identifying hatred, exclusion,
    and prejudice in, 15
  primary, 20, 21
  secondary and universal, 20–21,
22, 28
  symbolic importance of choice
    of, 44
  See also words
Lavrentije, Bishop, 87
Lebanon, war in, 64
Lederach, John Paul, 56–57
Liechty, Joseph, 10, 89–101, 127
local presence, importance of in
  peacebuilding projects, 85–86
losses, mourning of, 78–79
love, forgiveness as form of,
  100

Madrid Conference (1991), 64
Mapuche people, 124
Maya people, 122, 124
mercy, 54
Methodism, rhetoric and practice
  of, 97
Mexico, indigenous peoples in,
  124
Middle East, European colonial
  rule in, 68
Middle East conflict, 128
  compelling moral and historical
    claims by both sides, 64
  dialogue on between Jews,
    Christians, and Muslims, 10
  importance of Jerusalem in,
    40–41
  Israel/Palestine, 3, 40
    and principles of interfaith
      dialogue, 21–26
  peace process in, 63–65
    difficulties, 65
    importance of interfaith
      cooperation, 70–72
    issues for American Jews,
      66–67
    issues for Arab American
      Christians and Muslim
      Americans, 67–68

issues for non-Arab
American Christians,
68–70
role of Abrahamic religions in,
39–40
sacredness of land in, 40
suffering caused by, 64
See also Gaza; Israel; Palestine;
West Bank
Milimay, Haydee, 123
Miskito people, 124
mitigation, 91, 127
of anti-Catholicism, 97–101
Christian resources for, 99–100
definition of, 94
negotiating versus, 94–95
truth claims and, 101
using the tradition to heal the
tradition, 95
mob psychology, 39
Mojzes, Paul, 7
monotheistic relationship, shared
study and, 41–42
Montville, Joseph, 54
moral responsibility, acceptance of,
54
Moro (Philippines), 19
motivation, 17
Moving Beyond Sectarianism,
95–96
Moving Beyond Sectarianism
project, 91
murdered, inclusion of in religious
dialogue, 44
Muslim-Croat Federation, peace
building in, 86, 88
Muslims
beliefs and practices of, 22
in Bosnia-Herzegovina, 80–81,
85, 87, 108–109
Crusades as issue for, 17–18,
67–68
dialogue on Middle East with

Christians and Jews, 10, 21,
23
feelings during third phase of
dialogue, 28
in Kosovo, 110–111
message of bin Laden to, 3
Palestinian, 23–24
in the Philippines, 19
in U.S., Middle East issues and,
67–68
See also Islam
mythification, destructive, 42

Nahual people, 124
nakhba, 66–67
nationalism, as issue in interfaith
dialogue, 80–81, 106–107
NATO, in former Yugoslavia, 79,
88, 111
negotiation
external means of operation,
95
mitigation versus, 94–95
words during, 34
Nicaragua, indigenous peoples in,
124
Nikolaj, Metropolitan, 86
9/11. *See* September 11 terrorist
attacks
nonnegotiable beliefs, 92–94
difficulty of making them negotiable, 94
mitigation and, 94–95
Northern Ireland
anti-Catholicism in, 97–99
mitigation of, 99–101
Christianity in, 90
churches as socializing agents,
90
conflict in, 3
role of religion, 89–91
forgiveness practiced in,
100

Northern Ireland *(cont.)*
   mitigation of religious differ-
      ences in, 95–97, 100
   sectarianism in, 91

observer's role, in peacebuilding,
   73, 74
Oklahoma City federal building
   bombing, 67
Old Testament, 80–81
One Bread, One Body, 95–97
one world, interfaith dialogue as
   basis for creating, 6–7
oppression, protest of and resist-
   ance to, 15–16
Orange Order, 97–98
Orangeism, anti-Catholicism as
   part of, 98–99
Organization for Security and
   Cooperation in Europe
   (OSCE), 106, 108
OSCE. *See* Organization for
   Security and Cooperation in
   Europe (OSCE)
Oslo accords, 64
"other," the
   reconciliation with, 53–54
   stereotypes of, 49–50
Ottoman Empire, 67–68

Palestine
   Christians in, 23–24
   creation of Israel and, 66–67
   Hamas, 70
   holy sites in, 3
   liberation of, 64
   Lutheran bishop's appeal, 70
   self-determination of, 64, 66,
      69
   uprising in (1987), 64, 66
   violence in, 24–25
   See also Gaza; Middle East con-
      flict; West Bank

Palestine Liberation Organization
   (PLO)
   equated with terrorism, 69
   legitimacy of, 69
Palestinian Americans, Middle
   East issues and, 68
Pallas Athena, 125
Panama, indigenous peoples in,
   124
papal behavior, evaluation of, 43
participants in interfaith dialogue
   balance of power and, 22, 130
   decrease in number related to
      more progress, 38–39
   selection of, 22, 76, 130
Pasalic, Menšur, 74
peace constituency, 57
peacebuilding, 73
   clear purpose in, 75, 129
   defined, 56
   importance of local presence on
      the ground after, 85–86
   interfaith dialogue as tool for, 6,
      8–9, 9–10, 74–76
   effectiveness, 74–75
   essential follow-up measures,
      85–86
   guidelines, 76–85
   supportive institutional struc-
      tures, 86–88
   interreligious, 16
   intervention roles in, 73
   prerequisites for success, 75–76
   storytelling in context of,
      77–79
   URI involved in, 115–126
peacemaking
   dialogue in, 37
   importance of words in, 34
   interfaith dialogue and, 38
perception clarification exercises,
   80–81
Persian Gulf War, 67

personal experience, importance of examining, 77
Peru, indigenous peoples in, 124
Pius XII, Pope, 43
Pontanima Choir, 87
power
　balance of in interfaith dialogue, 21–22, 129
　imbalance of addressed, 21, 22, 23–24, 43
Prayer Vigil for the Earth (2000), 123
Presbyterianism, Westminster Confession, 97
primary language, 20, 21
Protestants
　anti-Catholicism among, 97–99
　evaluation of by Catholic Church, 95–97
　excluded from sharing communion with Catholics, 95–96, 96–97
　in Northern Ireland, 3
　difficulty of mitigating anti-Catholic beliefs, 97–99
　opposition to Belfast Agreement, 90
　Orange Order, 97–98
Psalms, lament motif in, 79

"Qualifications of an Orangeman, The," 98–99
Quichua people, 124
Qu'ran, 19, 22, 69
　righteousness articulated in, 51

Rabin, Yitzhak, 65
radio, use of in conflict resolution, 113
Rambachan, Anantanad, 55

reconciliation
　deeds of, 8, 10, 35–36, 37–38
　dialogue as, 35–36
　interfaith dialogue as part of, 8, 77
　methods of, 35–36
　strengthening one's own faith identity before attempting, 53
　sustaining over long periods, 52–53
　unreasonableness of immediate attempts at, 52–53
　words of, 35
religion
　common commandment to work for peace, 71
　contributions of to peace, 112–114
　exploring differences and developing tolerance in third phase of dialogue, 28
　as factor in international conflict, 3, 47–48, 105–106
　idealization of during first phase of dialogue, 27
　limitations of in influencing events, 111–112
　potential impact of as source of peacemaking, 16, 48
　recognizing similarities in second phase of dialogue, 27–28
　role of in Northern Ireland conflict, 89–91
　search for truth in, 55–56
Religion and Peacemaking Initiative (USIP), 9
religious beliefs, understanding one's own as basis for interfaith dialogue, 48–50
religious dialogue. *See* interfaith dialogue
religious differences
　as basis for conflict, 105

religious differences *(cont.)*
dealing with, 22–23, 129
difficulty of compromise on, 92–94
religious experience, depth of in interreligious interaction, 17–18
religious identity, 29
motivation from, 17
religious language, primary and secondary, 20–21, 22, 28
religious separation, versus social separation, 97
religious sites. *See* holy sites
religious study, shared, as part of interfaith exploration, 39–42, 44
revenge
exorcizing need for, 79, 130
forgiveness and, 82–83
right relationships, restoration of, 83
rituals
of forgiveness, 25
in interfaith dialogue, 18–19
scripture and sacred texts, 19
secondary and universal language versus primary language, 20–21
tension caused by use of, 20

sacred spaces. *See* holy sites
sacred texts, in interfaith dialogue, 19, 131
safe space, creation of, 78
Saje, Vjeko, 86
Sajlovic, Andjelko, 78
Sarajevo, siege of, 87–88
Sarajevo Phoenix, 88
Schneier, Arthur, 10, 105–114, 127
scriptures, in interfaith dialogue, 19
Second Vatican Council, 96, 97
secondary language, 20–21, 22, 28

sectarianism, in Northern Ireland, 91
segregation, 91
socializing into, 90
truth claims and, 91
September 11 terrorist attacks, 3–4
Serbia
Kosovo as part of, 110
peacebuilding in, 86
Serbian Orthodox church, 74, 82, 86, 87, 88, 108–109, 110–111
shame, 34
Shuar people, 124
similarities, examination of in interfaith dialogue, 22–23
sin
acknowledgment of by one's own group, 82
confession of, 81
mutual admission of, 10
social action, dialogue and, 15–16
Social Innovations in Global Management (SIGMA) program, 117
social separation, versus religious separation, 97
socialization, 90
South Africa, religious pursuit of justice during apartheid, 51–52
spirituality, in interfaith dialogue, 16–18
Steele, David, 10, 73–88, 128
stereotyping, forgiveness and, 83, 130
Stolov, Yehuda, 39, 40
"Stop the Destruction of Holy Sites" (UN resolution), 113
storytelling
to confront fears of the future, 79
impact of on reconciliation, 10, 77–79

as method of grieving losses,
78–79
study. *See* religious study
Swidler, Leonard, 6
Swing, William, 116
symbols, use of in reconciliation,
35, 36

Taize Community, 87
Taliban, 113
talk. *See* words
television, use of in conflict resolution, 113
terrorism
as motivation for interfaith dialogue, 5
religiously motivated, 5
September 11 attacks, 3–4
U.S. response to, 5
Tertullian, 92
"third culture," developed during
dialogue process, 18–19
Thirty-Nine Articles, the, 97
Torah, study of, 41–42
training
for religious diplomats and
peacemakers, 36–37
spirituality in, 17
transformation
interpersonal and structural, 56
of relationships, 36
as secondary goal to being faithful to God's purpose, 75
socioeconomic and political, 56
See also conflict transformation
traumatic experiences, recounting
of in storytelling, 77–79
tribalization, versus globalization, 107
truth
joint search for, 55–56
as pillar of interfaith dialogue,
55–56
truth claims, 91

mitigation and, 101
sectarianism and, 91
Turtle Island, First Peoples of, 125

Uganda
Cooperation Circles in, 120
interfaith dialogue in, 7
unireligious forums, 25–26, 48–50,
129
United Nations, 128
anniversary of charter signing,
116
in Bosnia, 108
"Stop the Destruction of Holy
Sites" resolution, 113
Summit of Religious and
Spiritual Leaders, 5–6
United Religions Initiative (URI),
10–11, 115, 128
in the Americas, 122–126
Brazil interfaith conference,
125–126
Buenos Aires summit, 123
charter, 115–116, 119
Cooperation Circles, 119,
120–121, 125
East Africa conference,
120–121
first global summit, 116, 118
foundational values, 119
global appreciative inquiry con-
ducted by, 118–119
as grassroots organization, 119
North America Regional
Summit, 125
Prayer Vigil for the Earth, 123
Quito conference, 124–125
United States
bombing of U.S. embassy in
Nairobi, 120–121
FBI targeting of Muslims and
Arab Americans during
Persian Gulf War, 67

United States *(cont.)*
  Jewish community in, 26
  Middle East issues
    for Arab American
      Christians, 67–68
    existing prejudices among
      different groups, 69
    history of persecution,
      intolerance, and colonial
      rule, 68–69
    ignorance of Palestinian suf-
      fering, 70
    for Jews, 66–67
    for Muslims, 67–68
    for non-Arab Christians,
      68–70
    for Palestinian Americans, 68
    public and political pro-Israel
      bias, 67
September 11 terrorist attacks, 3–4
United States Institute of Peace,
  4, 11
  advocacy of religious dialogue,
    4–5
  Religion and Peacemaking
    Initiative, 9
universal language, 20–21, 22–23
universalism, as part of second lan-
  guage, 22–23
URI. *See* United Religions
  Initiative (URI)
U.S. Interreligious Committee for
  Peace in the Middle East, 63,
  65

values, shared
  among different religions, 39
  importance of in interfaith peace
    building, 84–85
Vatican
  Congregation for the Doctrine
    of the Faith, 96
  Second Vatican Council, 96, 97

See also Catholic Church
victimization, sense of, 77, 130
violence, conflict-related, 91
Vivekananda, Swami, 55
voiceless, inclusion of in religious
  dialogue, 44

Weatherhead School of
  Management (Case Western
  University), 116–117
West Bank
  interfaith leadership trips to, 65
  Israeli occupation of, 68
  U.S. Jews' beliefs about, 66
  See also Gaza; Middle East con-
    flict; Palestine
Westminster Confession, 97
Wink, Walter, 100
words
  healing, 35, 131
  religious, 34–35
  use of to move closer to peace,
    34
  versus deeds of reconciliation, 8,
    10, 33–34, 37, 131
World Business Academy, 125
World Conference on Religion
  and Peace, 4, 76–77, 128
wrongdoing, acknowledging and
  healing, 8, 25, 81–82

Yakar Institute, 39
Young, Ronald, 10, 63–72, 128
Yugoslavia, former
  Appeal of Conscience opera-
    tions in, 107–108
  NATO bombing of, 79, 88
  peacebuilding in, 73–88
  See also individual nations

zakat, 22
Zionism, 69

INTERFAITH DIALOGUE AND PEACEBUILDING

This book is set in American Caslon; the display type is Apple Chancery. The Creative Shop designed the book's cover; Mike Chase designed the interior and made up the pages. David Sweet copyedited the text, which was proofread by Karen Stough. The index was prepared by Sonsie Conroy. The book's editor was Nigel Quinney.